DOCTORING PHOTOS WITH

Adobe® Photoshop®

LEARN THE TECHNIQUES OF THE PROS

BEFORE

AFTER

BEFORE

AFTER

BEFORE

AFTER

Eric Grebler

PHOTOSHOP MAKEOVER

Why spend thousands on plastic surgery, gym memberships, and salon bills? You can give yourself a Photoshop makeover in minutes with these easy-to-follow techniques.

PIMP YOUR RIDE

Want to impress others with your completely tricked-out car? Add dozens of special effects, modifications, and customizations to your ride and be the envy of all your friends.

FUN WITH PHOTOS

Who amongst us hasn't wanted to switch faces with someone else? You can accomplish this along with many other photo-altering techniques using the step-by-step instructions inside this book.

COVERS VERSIONS

| 7 | CS | CS2 |

Edited by Denise Miller.
Layout by Patricia Ann Wilkinson.

info@mimosabooks.com

ISBN 097353284X

For Kara and Ethan.

CONTENTS

Section I : Photoshop Makeover

Why spend thousands of dollars on plastic surgery, gym memberships, and salon bills? You can give yourself a Photoshop-style makeover in minutes using these easy-to-follow techniques.

Project 1: The Three Minute Hair Color Miracle

Getting your hair color just right is not only a difficult task, it can also prove to be very time-consuming and expensive. The beauty of this dye job is that you don't have to spend any time in the salon. There's no need to waste money on expensive treatments, and the best part is that you can accomplish this task in just a couple of minutes. By taking advantage of Photoshop's layer blending options, you'll see that you can create amazing results, such as the one in this photo -- literally in seconds. You'll be amazed at just how easy it is to get fast, realistic-looking results.

Project 2: Prom Makeover

Why is it that skin blemishes always seem to appear right before big events? No matter when or where they occur, blemishes can easily be removed in Photoshop. In this project, not only will we clear up the model's skin, we'll also apply some makeup and brighten up her lipstick. To apply the makeup we'll create a selection around her eyes and then adjust the hue levels. For the lipstick, we'll use the Shadow/Highlight command that will brighten the color of her lips. Finally, we can also add the illusion of colored contacts, again by adjusting the hue levels.

Project 3: Instant Tattoo

Are you one of those people who always wanted to get a tattoo but wasn't ready to make the commitment? Are you afraid of the pain? Worried about how it'll look when it's done? Don't want to be 80 years old and covered in tattoos? If you want to preview how a tattoo would look without having to make the commitment, then Photoshop is your answer. In this project, you'll create a tattoo from scratch and then apply it to a woman's arm. Once you get the hang of making and adjusting selections, you can create many types of wild and interesting shapes for your tattoos. Once the tattoo is created, you'll manipulate it to fit on the arm and then adjust the opacity to make it look realistic.

Project 4: Wardrobe Change

You get to work and you realize that your shirt doesn't really match your suit or your tie doesn't really fit in with your mood. Wouldn't it be nice if you could instantly change your wardrobe throughout the day without having to rush back home? The good news is that in the world of Photoshop, you can. There are about a dozen different ways you can change the colors of an object. Many of these ways will be explored throughout this book. In this project, we will change the color of clothing by using two different techniques. We'll change the color of one man's suit by using the Color Balance feature and adjust the other man's shirt by using the Hue/Saturation feature.

Project 5: Miracle Wrinkle Cream

There is a lyric from a Cher song that goes, "If I could turn back time, if I could find a way...." Well Cher, now you can turn back time using Photoshop. There is a billion dollar industry built around making people look younger. Whether it's surgery, creams, ointments, or masks, people will do just about anything to remove their wrinkles. This project will show you how to get rid of those unsightly lines in minutes without spending a dime. By creatively using the blur technique, we will soften all the lines on this man's face to make him look years younger.

Project 6: Growing Old Unnaturally

To be completely honest with you, there aren't a lot of people demanding a project that will make them look older. That being said, there's no better way to get revenge on an enemy or someone you simply don't like than by aging them. So, whether you want to get back at someone or you want to look into the crystal ball to see what you might look like ten to fifteen years down the line, you can follow the steps of this project. This project uses mostly drawing tools to enhance and lengthen laugh lines and wrinkles. It also uses the Burn tool to create some realistic-looking aging spots.

Project 7: Superfan

There is a classic episode from the hit television show "Seinfeld" in which one of the character's boyfriends paints his face to go to a hockey game and shouts out "You suck, Messier!" Whether you've seen the episode or not, almost anyone who has attended a professional or amateur sporting event has witnessed the "Superfan" -- that person who takes the game and their passion for the team far too seriously. In this project, you can emulate that "Superfan" look with any photo. We'll use a maple leaf image that was downloaded from the Internet as our template for painting on the makeup.

Project 8: Trading Faces

As disturbing as these images are, this is one of my favorite projects. The question I probably get most often when I teach people Photoshop is, "How can I put my face on someone else's body?" Well, you'll find the answer to this question in this project. The key to switching faces lies in matching the skin tones. To accomplish this, we'll adjust the hue levels and the brightness of the skin. After that, we'll adjust the opacity of the layers to help them blend with one another. Once you get the hang of this technique, you'll be switching faces of all of the members of your family, friends, and coworkers.

Section II : Pimp Your Ride

Want to impress others with your tricked-out ride? Add dozens of special effects, modifications and customizations to your car and be the envy of all of your friends.

Project 9: Tinted Windows

There's a line from a famous hip hop song by a group called Run-DMC that goes "tinted windows don't mean nothin', we know who's inside." If you think contrary to the band and like the idea of tinting your windows, you can do so virtually in Photoshop. When you get your windows tinted in real life, you have to make a commitment to the level of tint you want. This isn't the case in Photoshop, as you can adjust the brightness and contrast levels to get the desired tint level. This project will teach you some of the basics of making and adjusting selections.

Project 10: Turn On Your Headlights

Several years ago, laws were passed in almost every state requiring that all new cars must have daytime running lights. Ultimately, having your lights on all the time is simple a safer way to drive. If you happen to have an older model car, don't worry. You can create the illusion of illuminated lights by using Photoshop. Not only will we turn on the main highlights, we will also add a yellow glow to the fog lamps of this vehicle. We'll be using two different techniques for adding light to this vehicle. For the headlamps, we are going to apply a Lens Flare filter and for the fog lamps, we are going to simply adjust the color and change the brightness levels.

Project 11: Car Chameleon

There are dozens of auto body shops that will paint your car for you, but how many will guarantee that they'll have your car back to you in 5 minutes? How can you change the color of an object in Photoshop? Let me count the ways. In this project, we'll be using the Replace Color feature to change the color of the car. The Replace Color command simply allows you to pick a specific color to use as a replacement for an existing color. After you've finished coloring the car, you'll tidy up the selection by using the Eraser tool.

Project 12: Auto Detailing

Do you remember back in school when you would use a stencil to paint numbers and letters onto paper? We'll be using the same type of approach when applying the flames decal to our car in this project. We basically create a stencil out of an image of flames that was downloaded from the Internet. From there, we will fill the stencil with a color and modify it slightly so that it fits onto our car. This project is surprisingly easy and has some fantastic results. The real beauty of this project is that you can use the same steps described to apply other types of decals to an image of your car. Once you've mastered the steps, try downloading other decals to create different patterns on your photos.

Project 13: Convertible Conversion

Have you always dreamed of having a convertible? I've had one; and trust me -- they are not all they are cracked up to be. Where I live, there are only three months of the year during which you could actually have the top down. Of those three months, there are only a handful of days when it wouldn't be too scorchingly hot to drive topless. What's the solution? Create a virtual convertible in Photoshop with no large body shop bill involved. With a little help from the Clone Stamp tool, you'll be able to replicate the background after you've removed the roof.

Project 14: Reflection

Greek mythology tells us the story of Narcissus, a young man who falls in love with his own reflection. If you have a photograph of a sweet car like the one pictured here, you may want to create a reflection so that it too can fall in love with itself. The process of creating a reflection is really quite simple. The reflection itself is just a slightly modified copy of the original image. After you've selected and copied the image, you will flip it and then change its opacity to make the reflection look authentic. This technique is also great to use on images of landscapes and skylines.

Project 15: Need For Speed

Scientific studies have shown that certain people who love risk-taking and danger have an imbalance of an enzyme called MAO. For the rest of us, who are afraid of great risks but still want to create the illusion of danger and speed, we can follow this project. Here we will create the illusion of motion by applying a blur filter. We are also going to create artificial smoke, billowing from the tires, and the look of acceleration. You can apply the techniques in this project to just about any photograph of a motionless car, boat, motorcycle, or person.

Section III : Fun With Photos

Photoshop provides you with a myriad of tools that will allow you to do just about anything with your photos. In this section, we'll stretch the limits of our imagination, performing all types of experiments with our photos.

Project 16: Hockey Fight

Growing up in Canada, whether we liked it or not, we were exposed in some way to hockey. Whether it was watching Hockey Night in Canada on Saturday nights, early morning hockey practices, or playing at the outdoor rink after school, hockey was part of life for most Canadian kids. Fortunately for me, my father kept me out of contact hockey so I could escape the bumps, bruises, and fights that some of my friends had to endure. Even though I avoided the fights, I can still create the illusion of the results of a hockey battle by using the various tools in Photoshop. I can guarantee that after completing this project, no Tylenol or bandages will be required.

103

Project 17: You Too Can Be Famous

My wife loves everything to do with celebrities. She loves watching them on entertainment TV shows, she loves reading about them in magazines, and above all she loves having her picture taken with them. I, on the other hand, couldn't be bothered with chasing after those that appear on TV. With this project, we both win, because I can put myself into a photo of any celebrity without having to chase them down or bother them. In this project you'll not only learn the techniques used to extend a photograph to make room for yourself, you'll learn some techniques for making the doctored photograph look realistic.

111

Project 18: Breaking Up Is Easy To Do

There's really nothing much worse than the process of going through a breakup with someone. The pictures of you and your mate around the house are constant reminders of how something so right, went so wrong. The problem with throwing out those photos is that you just look so darn good in some of those shots, and it would be a crying shame to waste them. Not to worry - Photoshop to the rescue! In Photoshop you can remove unwanted elements, including people, with relative ease. There are a variety of tools that you can use to remove an object and then replace it with other elements of the background. This project primarily uses the Patch and Clone Stamp tools to replicate the background and remove the unwanted man.

121

Project 19: Be Your Own Comic Book Hero

Do you have a favorite comic book hero? Is it Spiderman? Batman? Wonder Woman? The real heroes in life are all around us -- our friends, coworkers, family, and neighbors. Using Photoshop, you can make anyone into a comic book hero simply by applying a few filters. Filters act as special effects that you can apply to a photograph that will allow you, amongst other things, to convert any person into a comic book character. If you are using versions CS or CS2, you can use the Filter Gallery, which allows you to apply multiple filters without having to access different dialog boxes. If you are using version 7 you will have to apply these filters one at a time.

125

Project 20: Create Your Own Old-Fashioned Photo

I'm sure that somewhere in your house you've got a box of old photographs that have begun to show the signs of aging. So much attention is given to fixing and converting old photographs to make them look new. But what if you want to go the other way around? Through the use of a variety of effects and features, Photoshop gives you all the tools you need to make a new photograph look old. Why wait decades for a photo to become tattered-looking and aged, when you can accomplish the same effect in seconds?

Project 21: Gnome In A Bottle

If you take a second look at the image on the right, you'll notice that inside the clear bottle is a garden gnome. The trick to this project is making the gnome appear as if it is actually inside the bottle. After isolating and copying the gnome from a different image, you'll paste and resize him into the image of the bottles. Then, by copying and pasting certain elements of the bottle, you'll create the illusion that he is actually within the bottle. To finalize the look, you'll adjust the layer opacity to really make the gnome look like he is behind glass.

Project 22: Neon Sign

I used to attend a sign show every year as the staff member of a popular graphics application vendor. No matter what year it was, 80% of the questions I would receive involved how to create the illusion of neon in a graphic. Many of the attendees were sign manufacturers who needed to show their customers a preview of how a sign would look before it was actually created. By taking advantage of layer styles, you can apply a realistic neon effect to just about any object. Once the neon is applied, it can be tweaked to adjust the color and intensity.

Project 23: Turn A Photo Into A Sketch

If you're a TV junkie like me, you may recall a show from the early '90s called Blossom. Just prior to going to a commercial break, the show would freeze, and the frozen image would be converted to a sketch. That's exactly what we'll be doing in this project. We'll take a photograph, and, following a few steps, we'll convert our image into a colored sketch. This project makes use of several of the built-in filters of Photoshop. These filters allow you to apply a myriad of special effects to your images. With a bit of tweaking, you can convert just about any photograph to a colored sketch. In this project, we'll be converting an image of a flag; but the technique also works very well with pictures of landscapes, flowers, and abstracts.

Project 24: Change Of Scene

I recently had a pool installed at my house. And it's funny, because after the installation I have become an instant meteorologist. I always need to know what the forecast is so that I can plan out my activities. Wouldn't it be nice if we didn't need to be so dependent on the weather and we could change the forecast to suit our needs? The good news is that in Photoshop you can! In this project, we'll replace one sky with another. Rather than taking the new sky from an existing image, we will actually create it from scratch using Photoshop's Render Clouds feature. By creating a selection with the Magic Wand tool, we can remove the existing sky and put in our newly created background.

159

Project 25: Monkey Face

Who amongst us hasn't wanted to play the role of God—being all-powerful and having the ability to create anything you'd like? In this project, you'll get to do some experimenting as if you were all-knowing and all-powerful. There are two keys to getting a realistic look to the animal. The first is that, when isolating the monkey's head, you capture parts of the fur on the face that are sticking out. To accomplish this, you will use the Extract feature that was first introduced in Photoshop CS. The second key is that you must resize and position the monkey's head so that it fits in perspective with that of the original animal. When you are finished, you should be left with your new species!

163

Project 26: Extreme Diving

Isn't it funny how every four years, whenever the Summer Olympics come along, we all of a sudden take interest in sports that we would never give a second thought to otherwise? Diving is one such sport for me; but I will say that, depending on the venue, you can get some spectacular views of the city from the top diving board. In this project, we are going to create the illusion of one of these spectacular views by transporting the image of the diver over a city scape. There are many different isolation techniques that we can use in Photoshop to remove an object from an image, and in this case, we'll be using a technique called layer masking.

169

Project 27: Hair Transplant

I'm sure that you've seen the ad for a popular hair restoration clinic, in which the spokesman says, "I'm not only the owner, I'm also a client." While there are literally hundreds of hair loss treatments on the market, none seem to work 100% -- except perhaps one. That one, of course, is Photoshop. In this project you'll simply be transplanting hair from one image to another. We'll soften the edges of the hair, to make it look more realistic by using the feathering option while creating the selection. After we've copied and pasted the selection of hair, we'll reposition it on the photo of the man.

175

Project 28: Operation Rhino Drop

For those of you who are old enough to remember, you may recall a Disney movie from 1995 entitled "Operation Dumbo Drop." In the movie, an army troop goes through a series of high jinks while trying to transport an elephant during the Vietnam War in order to retain the loyalty of a local village. It's much easier to move large animals in Photoshop than in real life. In this project, we'll take a picture of a rhinoceros in his local habitat and paste it into the Egyptian pyramids. To make the photo more interesting, we'll make it seem as though the rhinoceros is gigantic and that it is stepping over the pyramid.

Project 29: Now Appearing In Color

I'm sure at one point or another that you've walked past a photo-developing store in your local mall where they offered the service of having your old photos converted from black and white to color. Aside from the small fortune that you could save by doing it yourself, you'll find that Photoshop makes this process extremely easy. Once you get the hang of it, you can try hundreds of different color combinations to get colors that are right for you. This project uses several different coloring and selection techniques. The one that you ultimately end up using will depend on your preferences and the end result that you wish to see on screen.

Project 30: See Yourself In Pumpkin

Have you ever wondered how people create those incredible, life-like carvings out of their pumpkins at Halloween? Well, wonder no longer - it's really quite simple. You can take just about any photograph and convert it to a black and white image that can be used as a template when carving a pumpkin. In this project, you'll not only create a template, you'll also apply the template to a picture of a pumpkin so that you can preview how it will look before you start carving. Say goodbye to simple triangle eyes and zig-zagged mouth pumpkins. During this Halloween, your jack-o-lantern will be the envy of the block.

Project 31: KISS Cat

You can tell at first glance that this cat wants to "…rock and roll all night, and party every day…." The best part of this project is taking advantage of the Liquify feature, which allows you to make the cat appear as though it is smiling. Think of the Liquify feature as giving you the ability to convert your photo paper into a gel-like substance that can easily be molded. Through simple copying and pasting, you are going to also make the cat appear as if it has a mohawk. We'll also make our cat look like Paul Stanley of KISS by applying a star to its eye. After you finish this project, I suggest that you experiment with the Liquify feature on other photos of animals and people. It's guaranteed to give you hours of entertainment.

The Three Minute
Hair Color
Miracle

Getting your hair color just right is not only a difficult task it can also prove to be very time-consuming and expensive. The beauty of this dye job is that you don't have to spend any time in the salon. There's no need to waste money on expensive treatments and the best part is that you can accomplish this task in just a couple of minutes. By taking advantage of Photoshop's layer blending options, you'll see that you can create amazing results, such as the one in this photo – literally in seconds. You'll be amazed at just how easy it is to get fast, realistic-looking results.

Project Files

The file for this project is called hair color.tif and can be found at:
www.mimosabooks.com/files

Completion Time

After the files have been downloaded, this project should take approximately five minutes to ten minutes to complete.

Degree of Difficulty

☆

Project Tools

Brush Tool

Palettes

Ensure the following palettes, which can be accessed from the Window menu, are open for this project:

Tools
Navigator
Layers
Colors

STEP 1 : OPEN THE TUTORIAL

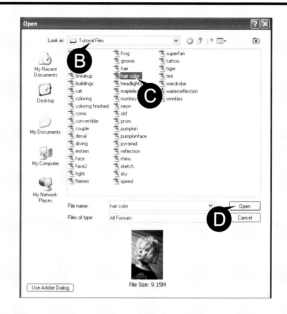

Before we can get any work done, we need to first open the files we'll need for this project.

A. Press Ctrl+O (PC) or Command+O (Mac) to launch the Open dialog box.

B. Browse to the folder where you saved the tutorial files.

C. Click on the file entitled "hair color.tif." It will be highlighted.

D. Click the Open button. The file will open.

STEP 2 : VIEWING THE FILE

In order to work with this file, we should maximize the window and zoom into the area surrounding the hair.

A. Click the Maximize button to expand the window. This will make it easier to isolate the hair.

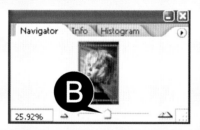

B. Click and drag the Zoom slider in the Navigator palette to zoom into the area around the hair. A zoom level of approximately 26% should suffice.

STEP 3 : DUPLICATING THE LAYER

Rather than working on the background layer, we'll create a copy of the image to manipulate. We will then manipulate the copy to change the color of the woman's hair.

A. Press Ctrl+J on the keyboard (PC) or Command+J (Mac) to create a duplicate of the Background layer. By default, the new layer will be selected.

STEP 4 : PAINTING THE HAIR

Here's the tough part of this project, and the good news is that it's not tough at all. By using the Brush tool, you simply paint over the woman's hair. There's no need to be very precise or accurate -- just paint away. You'll select the brush color prior to painting.

A. Click the Brush Tool button.

B. Click the Brush Preset picker. A dialog box will appear from which you can adjust the brush size.

C. Click and drag the Master Diameter slider to adjust the brush size. A brush size of approximately 70px should suffice.

D. Click and drag the R slider in the Color palette until the value is approximately 224.

E. Paint over the woman's hair.

F. Repeat Steps B and C to increase or decrease the size of the brush as you paint.

G. Continue painting until the hair is completely covered.

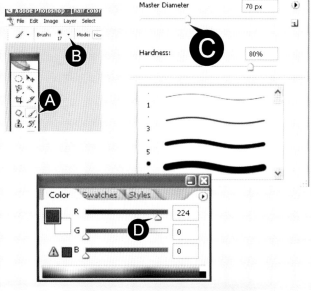

STEP 5 : BLENDING THE LAYERS

The picture looks a little ridiculous at this point as there is just a solid red blob over the woman's hair. To make it look realistic, we will blend Layer 1 with the Background layer. The results will amaze you!

A. Click on the Blend Mode arrow. A pop-up menu for blending layers will appear.

B. Click the Hue option. Just like that -- the color will blend based on the hue levels and the blond woman will now be a pink-head.

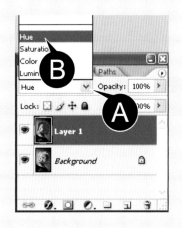

Prom
Makeover

2

Why is it that skin blemishes always seem to appear right before big events? No matter when or where they occur, blemishes can easily be removed in Photoshop. In this project, not only will we clear up the model's skin, we'll also apply some makeup and brighten up her lipstick. To apply the makeup we'll create a selection around her eyes and then adjust the hue levels. For the lipstick, we'll use the Shadow/Highlight command that will brighten the color of her lips. Finally, we can also add the illusion of colored contacts, again by adjusting the hue levels.

Project Files

The file for this project is called prom.tif and can be found at:
www.mimosabooks.com/files

Completion Time

After the files have been downloaded, this project should take approximately ten minutes to fifteen minutes to complete.

Degree of Difficulty

☆☆☆

Project Tools

🔍 Zoom Tool

🔲 Crop Tool

🔾 Lasso Tool

◯ Patch Tool

Palettes

Ensure the following palettes, which can be accessed from the Window menu, are open for this project:

Tools

Layers

STEP 1 : OPEN THE TUTORIAL

Before we can get any work done, we need to first open the file we'll be using in this project.

A. Press Ctrl+O (PC) or Command+O (Mac) to launch the Open dialog box.

B. Browse to the folder where you saved the tutorial files.

C. Click on the file entitled "prom.tif." It will be highlight-ed.

D. Click the Open button. The file will open.

E. Click the Maximize button to expand the window to its full size.

F. Press Ctrl+J (PC) or Command+J (Mac) to create a working layer.

STEP 2 : REMOVING THE BLEMISH

There's no better way to describe the Patch tool other than "amazing." It's the perfect tool for removing minor flaws in a photo while keeping its integrity.

A. Click the Zoom Tool button.

B. Click and drag around the area that contains the blem-ish.

C. Click and hold the button under the Crop Tool button. A list of buttons will appear. These buttons will vary depend-ing on which version of Photoshop you are using.

D. Click the Patch Tool option.

E. Click and drag around the blemish. When you release the mouse button, a selection marquee will appear around the blemish.

F. Position the mouse pointer over the selection. The mouse pointer will have a small rectangle attached to it.

G. Click and drag the selection to a clear area of the cheek. When you release the mouse button, the blemish will disappear.

H. Press Ctrl+D (PC) or Command+D (Mac) to remove the selection.

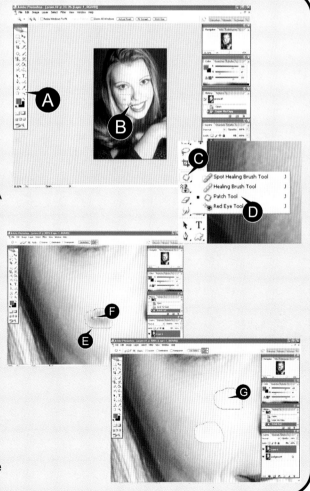

STEP 3 : CHANGING THE EYE COLOR

Photoshop provides a myriad of ways to change the color of an object, but one of the simplest is to select an area and adjust the hue levels. Here we will make the model's eyes blue.

A. Hold down the Space bar. Click and drag downward until the model's eyes are in view. As the Space Bar is pressed, the mouse pointer will turn into a hand.

B. Click the Lasso Tool button.

C. Click the "New selection" button on the options bar.

D. Click and drag around the colored part of the model's right eye.

E. Click the "Add to selection" button.

F. Click and drag around the colored part of the models's left eye.

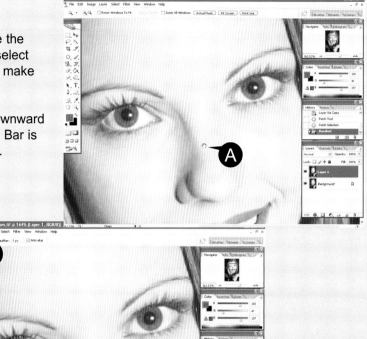

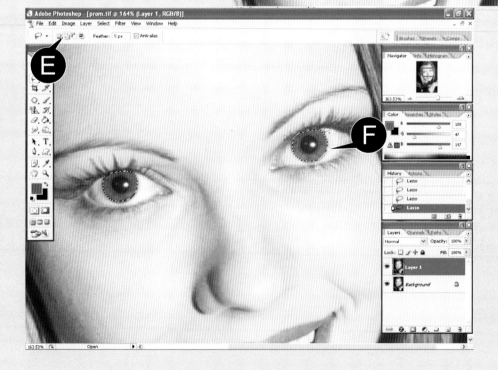

STEP 3 : CHANGING THE EYE COLOR CONT.

G. Click the "Subtract from selection" button. We'll use this to remove the pupils from the selection.

H. Click and drag around both pupils individually. They will be removed from the selection.

I. Press Ctrl+U (PC) or Command+U (Mac) to bring up the Hue/Saturation dialog box.

J. Click and drag the sliders to adjust the settings as follows: Hue: +180, Saturation: +25, Lightness: +10.

K. Click OK. The eyes will now be blue.

L. Press Ctrl+D (PC) or Command+D (Mac) to remove the selection.

M. Press Ctrl+0 (PC) or Command+0 (Mac) to zoom to full view.

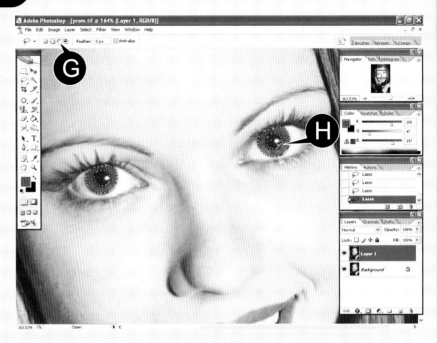

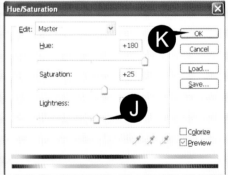

Once you have created a selection, you can move it by pressing the arrow keys on your keyboard. Each time that you press an arrow, the selection will move one pixel at a time.

STEP 4 : BRIGHTENING

To brighten the model's lipstick we'll make use of the Shadows and Highlights function.

A. Click the Zoom Tool button.

B. Click and drag around the model's mouth.

C. Click the Lasso Tool button.

D. Click the "New selection" button on the options bar.

E. Click and drag around the outside of the model's lips.

F. Click the "Subtract from selection" button. We'll use this to remove the teeth from the selection.

G. Click and drag around the model's teeth. They will be removed from the selection.

H. Click Image | Adjustments | Shadow/Highlight. The Shadow/Highlight dialog box will open.

I. Click and drag the sliders to set the following: Shadows Amount: 0, Highlights Amount: 20.

J. Click OK. The model's lips will appear as if lipstick has been applied.

K. Press Ctrl+D (PC) or Command+D (Mac) to remove the selection.

L. Press Ctrl+0 (PC) or Command+0 (Mac) to zoom to full view.

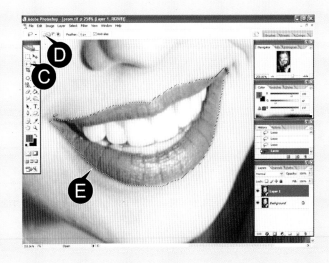
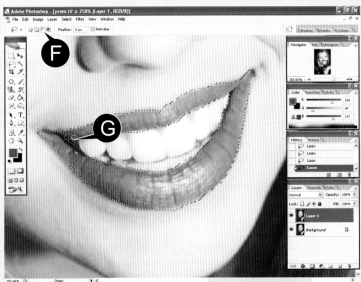
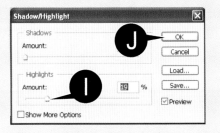

STEP 5 : ADDING MAKEUP

To apply diva-style makeup to this woman, we'll use the same technique we used to change her eye color. After selecting the area to which the makeup will be applied, we'll create a new layer, adjust the colors, and then play with the layer blending.

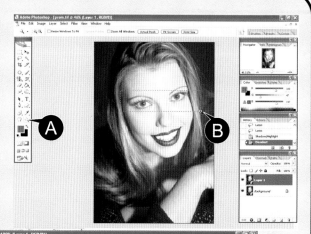

A. Click the Zoom Tool button.

B. Click and drag around the model's eyes.

C. Click the Lasso Tool button.

D. Click the "New selection" button on the options bar.

E. Enter "5" in the Feather box.

F. Click and drag around the model's right eye, starting from under her eyebrows and going to just below her eye.

G. Click on the "Add to selection" button.

H. Repeat Step F for the left eye.

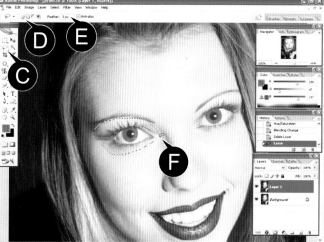

STEP 5 : ADDING MAKEUP CONT.

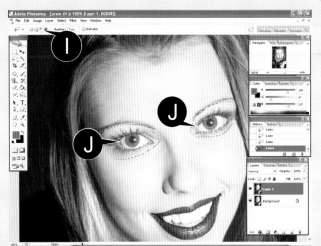

I. Click the "Subtract from selection" button. We'll use this to remove the eye from the selection.

J. Click and drag around the model's eyes individually. They will be removed from the selection.

K. Press Ctrl+J (PC) or Command+J (Mac) to create a new layer from the selection.

L. Press Ctrl+U (PC) or Command+U (Mac) to bring up the Hue/Saturation dialog box.

M. Click and drag the sliders to set the following levels: Hue: -100, Saturation -5, Lightness: +10.

N. Click OK to close the dialog box and apply the settings.

O. Click the Blend Mode button in the Layers palette.

P. Click Multiply. The layers will be blended.

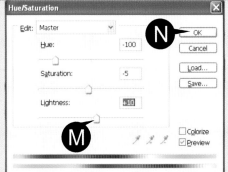

Instant
Tattoo

Are you one of those people who always wanted to get a tattoo but wasn't ready to make the commitment? Are you afraid of the pain? Worried about how it'll look when it's done? Don't want to be 80 years old and covered in tattoos? If you want to preview how a tattoo would look without having to make the commitment, then Photoshop is your answer. In this project, you'll create a tattoo from scratch and then apply it to a woman's arm. Once you get the hang of making and adjusting selections, you can create many types of wild and interesting shapes for your tattoos. Once the tattoo is created, you'll manipulate it to fit on the arm and then adjust the opacity to make it look realistic.

Project Files

The file for this project is called tattoo.tif and can be found at:
www.mimosabooks.com/files

Completion Time

After the files have been downloaded, this project should take approximately ten minutes to fifteen minutes to complete.

Degree of Difficulty

☆☆☆

Project Tools

⬚ Elliptical Marquee Tool

⬚ Move Tool

⬚ Magic Wand Tool

Palettes

Ensure the following palettes, which can be accessed from the Window menu, are open for this project:

Tools

Layers

STEP 1 : OPEN THE TUTORIAL

Before we can get any work done, we need to first open the file we'll be using in this project.

A. Press Ctrl+O (PC) or Command+O (Mac) to launch the Open dialog box.

B. Browse to the folder where you saved the tutorial files.

C. Click on the file entitled "tattoo.tif." It will be high-lighted.

D. Click the Open button. The file will open.

E. Click the Maximize button to expand the window to fit the screen.

F. Press Ctrl+0 (PC) or Command+0 (Mac) to fit the image to the screen.

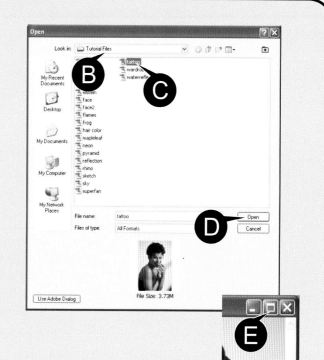

PHOTOGRAPHY 101

The Rule of Thirds - One of the most basic, yet important principles of photography is the rule of thirds. This rule deals with the alignment of objects in your photograph. The common thought is to simply align your subject so that it will be in the center of the photograph. This, however, goes against the rule of thirds. To apply the rule of thirds, you have to imagine that your photograph is divided into thirds both horizontally and vertically. The easiest way to imagine this is to picture that three horizontal and three vertical lines are running through your photograph. The four locations where the lines intersect are your "subject zones." In the image seen here, these "subject zones" are illustrated by four red circles. It's in these zones that you should align the key elements of your photograph. While you don't have to follow the rule of thirds for every shot, it's a good idea to get into the habit of following it for most of your pictures.

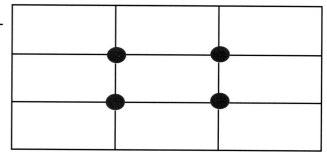

STEP 2 : CREATING THE TATTOO

We are going create the tattoo from scratch in a new document.

A. Press Ctrl+N (PC) or Command+N (Mac) to bring up the New dialog box.

B. Type 300 into the Width, Height and Resolution fields. All the units of measurements for the these three should be pixels.

C. Click OK. A new blank document will appear.

D. Click and hold the Rectangular Marquee Tool button. A list of options will appear.

E. Click the Elliptical Marquee Tool option.

F. Click and drag starting from near the top left corner to the bottom right to create an elliptical selection.

G. Click the "Subtract from selection" button on the options bar.

H. Position the mouse pointer up and to the left of the selection.

I. Click and drag downward and to the right so that the two elliptical objects are overlapping with a half moon shape remaining at the bottom. When you release the mouse button, you'll be left with a half-moon shape.

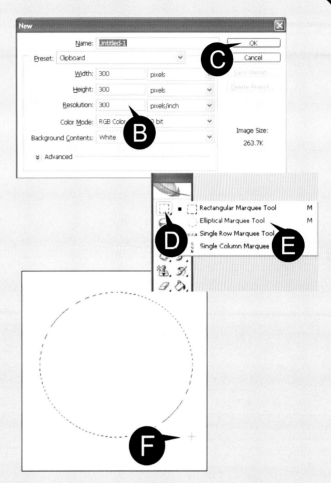

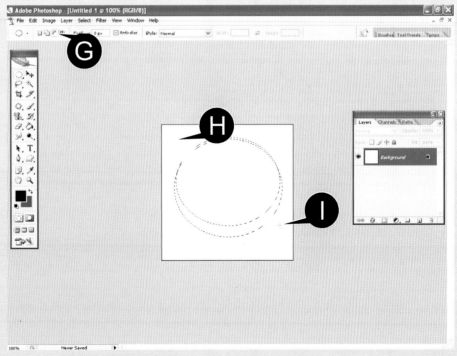

STEP 3 : FILLING THE SELECTION

The next step is to fill the half-moon selection with some color. We'll do this by using the Fill command.

A. Click Edit | Fill. The Fill dialog box will appear.

B. Click the arrow beside the Use box to see a list of fill options.

C. Click Color. The Color dialog box will appear.

D. Click on the color "black" or enter 0 in the R, G, and B fields.

E. Click OK. You'll return to the Fill dialog box.

F. Click OK. The selection will be filled with black.

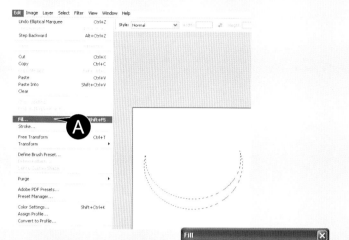

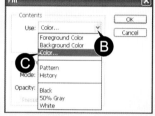

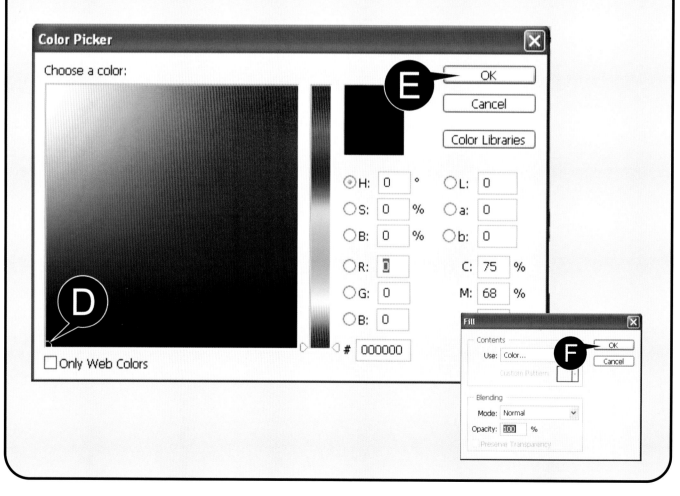

STEP 4 : MAKING THE TATTOO

In order to make the tattoo we are simply going to duplicate the shape we created several times and rotate it in different directions to create an interesting shape.

A. Press Ctrl+J (PC) or Command+J (Mac) to make a layer from the selected area.

B. Click the Move Tool button. A series of handles will appear around the object.

C. Position the mouse pointer just outside the top right handle. You'll know you are in the right position when the mouse pointer turns into a curved, double-sided arrow.

D. Click and drag upward and to the left. As you drag, the shape will rotate. Continue dragging until the shape is completely flipped.

E. Press the Commit button on the options bar.

F. Press Ctrl+J (PC) or Command+J (Mac) to make a layer from the selected area.

G. Position the mouse pointer just outside the bottom right handle. You'll know you are in the right position when the mouse pointer turns into a curved, double-sided arrow.

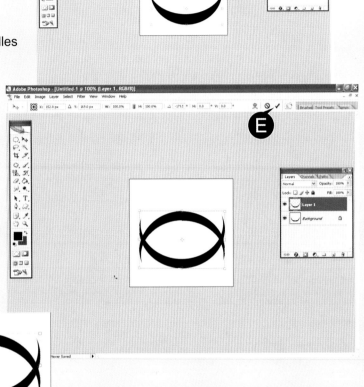

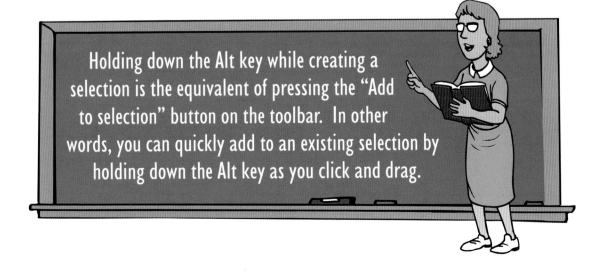

Holding down the Alt key while creating a selection is the equivalent of pressing the "Add to selection" button on the toolbar. In other words, you can quickly add to an existing selection by holding down the Alt key as you click and drag.

STEP 4 : MAKING THE TATTOO CONT.

H. Click and drag upward and to the left. As you drag the shape will rotate. Continue dragging until the shape has rotated 90 degrees.

I. Press the Commit button on the options bar.

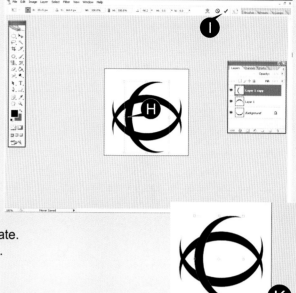

J. Press Ctrl+J (PC) or Command+J (Mac) to make a layer from the selected area.

K. Position the mouse pointer just outside the bottom right handle. You'll know you are in the right position when the mouse pointer turns into a curved, double-sided arrow.

L. Click and drag upward. As you drag the shape will rotate. Continue dragging until the shape has rotated 90 degrees.

M. Press the Commit button on the options bar.

N. Click Layer | Merge Visible. All of the layers will be combined together.

O. Press Ctrl+A (PC) or Command+A (Mac) to select the entire tattoo image.

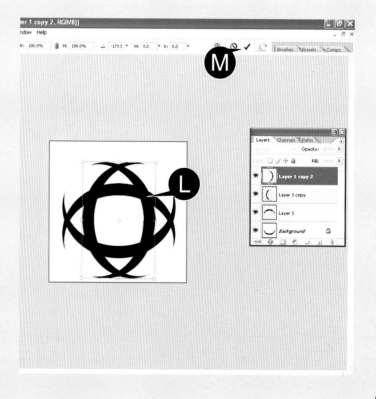

STEP 5 : IMPORTING THE TATTOO

To bring the tattoo into our photo image of the woman, we will simply copy and paste it. Once we have the tattoo in our image, we'll adjust it to make it look realistic. Part of the adjustment will be to remove the white background.

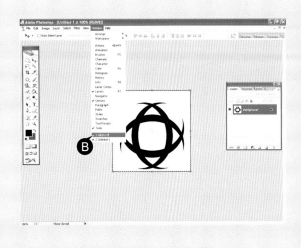

A. Press Ctrl+C (PC) or Command+C (Mac) to copy the tattoo.

B. Click Window | tattoo.tif. You'll switch to the image of the woman.

C. Press Ctrl+V (PC) or Command+V (Mac) to paste the tattoo.

D. Click the Move Tool button. A series of handles will appear around the tattoo.

E. Position the mouse pointer over the middle of the tattoo. Click and drag it until it is over the woman's shoulder.

F. Position the mouse pointer over the middle right handle. Click and drag inward slightly to squish the tattoo.

G. Repeat Step F with the middle left handle.

H. Click the Commit button on the options bar.

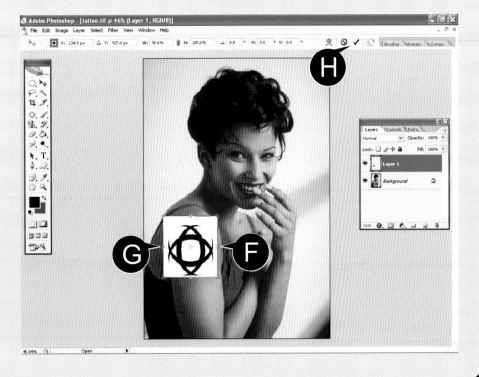

STEP 5 : IMPORTING THE TATTOO CONT.

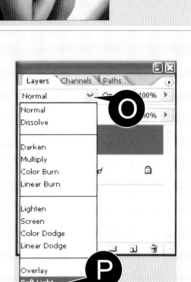

I. Click the Magic Wand Tool button.

J. Check the Anti-Alias box, if there is not already a checkmark in it. Make sure any of the other boxes in the options bar are not selected.

K. Click on any white area of the tattoo. A selection will be created.

L. Click Select | Grow. The selection will grow slightly.

M. Press the Delete key on the keyboard. The white portion of the tattoo will be removed.

N. Press Ctrl+D (PC) or Command+D (Mac) to remove the selection.

O. Click the Blend Mode button in the Layers palette.

P. Click the Soft Light option. The tattoo will now appear faded into the woman's arm.

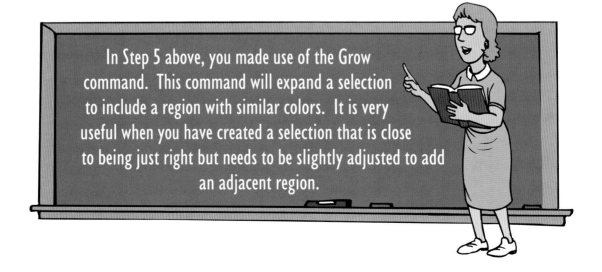

In Step 5 above, you made use of the Grow command. This command will expand a selection to include a region with similar colors. It is very useful when you have created a selection that is close to being just right but needs to be slightly adjusted to add an adjacent region.

Wardrobe
Change

You get to work and you realize that your shirt doesn't really match your suit or your tie doesn't really fit in with your mood. Wouldn't it be nice if you could instantly change your wardrobe throughout the day without having to rush back home? The good news is that in the world of Photoshop, you can. There are about a dozen different ways you can change the colors of an object. Many of these ways will be explored throughout this book. In this project, we will change the color of clothing by using two different techniques. We'll change the color of one man's suit by using the Color Balance feature and adjust the other man's shirt by using the Hue/Saturation feature.

Project Files

The file for this project is called wardrobe.tif and can be found at:
www.mimosabooks.com/files

Completion Time

After the files have been downloaded, this project should take approximately ten minutes to fifteen minutes to complete.

Degree of Difficulty

Project Tools

🔍   Zoom Tool

💠   Magnetic Lasso Tool

🔗   Lasso Tool

Palettes

Ensure the following palettes, which can be accessed from the Window menu, are open for this project:

Tools

Layers

STEP 1 : OPEN THE TUTORIAL

Before we can get any work done, we need to first open the file we'll need for this project.

A. Press Ctrl+O (PC) or Command+O (Mac) to launch the Open dialog box.

B. Browse to the folder where you saved the tutorial files.

C. Click on the file entitled "wardrobe.tif." It will be high-lighted.

D. Click the Open button. The file will open.

E. Press Ctrl+J (PC) or Command+J (Mac) to make a duplicate of the image on a separate layer. It's always a good idea to work on a duplicate rather than an original.

F. Click the Maximize button to have the window take up the entire screen.

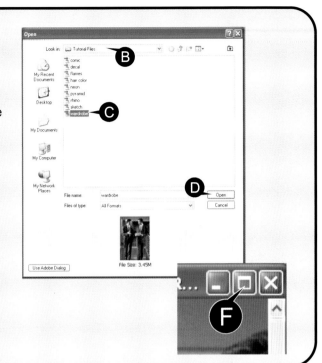

STEP 2 : CREATING A SELECTION

In order to change the color of the suit, we must first tell Photoshop where we would like to have the color change occur. We do this by creating a selection. A selection isolates a particular area so that you can make changes to that spot in the image without affecting other areas. To make our selection, we will use the Magnetic Lasso tool, which clings to certain areas like a magnet as you are creating your selection.

A. Press Ctrl+0 (PC) or Command+0 (Mac) to enlarge the picture so that it fits on the screen.

B. Click and hold the Lasso Tool button to see a list of different selection tools.

C. Click the Magnetic Lasso Tool option.

D. Click and drag around the outside edge of the suit of the man on the left. As you drag, a line with little nodes should cling to the edge of the man's suit. Don't worry if the line doesn't cling properly in all areas, as we'll fix any problems in the next step.

E. Double-click when you reach the point where you started. A selection, represented by a series of "marching ants," will appear around the suit.

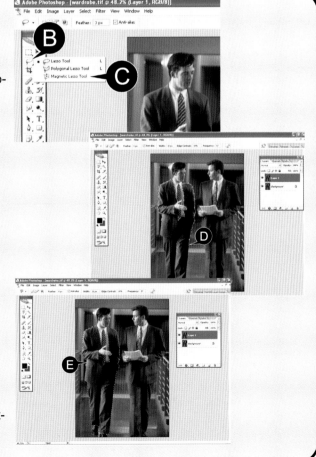

STEP 3 : ADJUSTING THE SELECTION

While the Magnetic Lasso tool did a great job of isolating the image, it isn't perfect. We'll use the Lasso tool to add to and subtract from different parts of our selection that need to be adjusted.

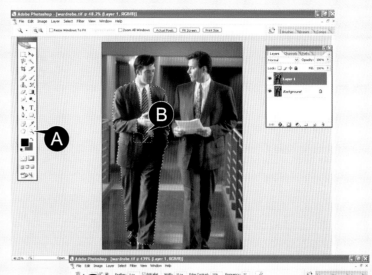

A.   Click the Zoom Tool button.

B. Click and drag around an area that needs to be included in the selection, but was missed when you first created the selection. You will now be zoomed in tight around that area.

C. Click and hold the Lasso Tool button to see a list of different selection tools.

D. Click the Lasso Tool option.

E. Click the "Add to selection" button in the toolbar. This will put you into "additive mode," so any area you drag around will be added to your selection.

F. Click and drag around an area that you would like to add to the selection. When you release your mouse button, the area around which you dragged will be added to the selection.

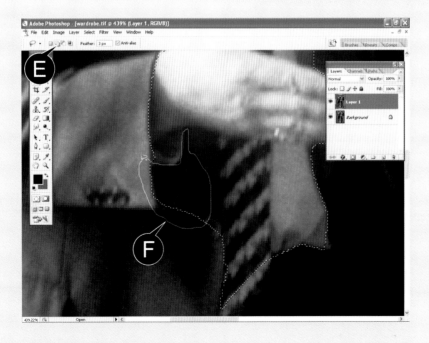

STEP 3 : ADJUSTING THE SELECTION CONT.

G. Press Ctrl+0 (PC) or Command+0 (Mac) to zoom out to full view again.

H. Repeat Steps A - G for any other areas you would like to add to your selection.

I. Click the "Subtract from selection" button in the options bar. This will put you into "subtractive mode," so any area that you drag around will be removed from your selection.

J. Click and drag around an area that you would like to remove from the selection. When you release your mouse button, the area around which you dragged will be removed from the selection. You may have to zoom in to get a better view. Steps A - B above cover how to zoom into a specific area.

K. Press Ctrl+0 (PC) or Command+0 (Mac) to zoom out to full view again.

L. Repeat Step J for any other areas you would like to remove from your selection.

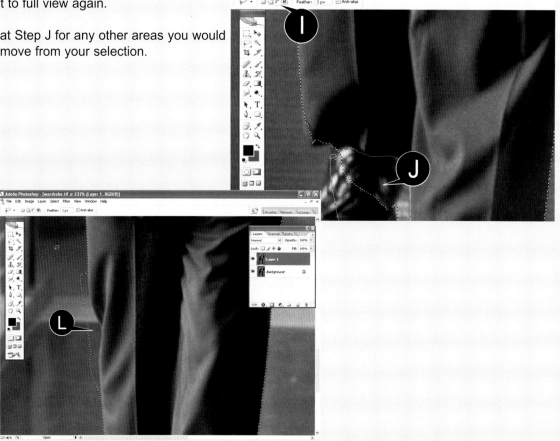

STEP 4 : CHANGING COLORS

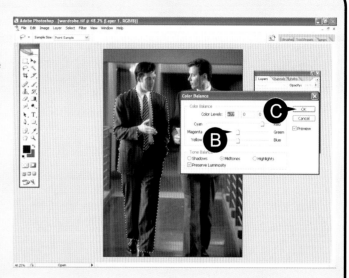

One of the many ways we can change the color of an object in Photoshop is to use the Color Balance dialog box. Depending on the color mode you are working in, an image is usually made up of either cyan, yellow, magenta and black or red, green and blue. The Color Balance dialog box allows you to adjust the levels of these colors.

A. Press Ctrl+B (PC) or Command+B (Mac) to bring open the Color Balance dialog box.

B. Click and drag the Red slider until it reaches 77. Ensure the Green and Blue sliders remain at 0. The suit will now have a reddish, purplish color. All the shades will remain but the color will change.

C. Click OK. The suit color will now be changed.

D. Press Ctrl+D (PC) or Command+D (Mac) to deselect your selection.

PHOTOGRAPHY 101

Make Eye Contact - When taking photographs, it's important that you get down (or up) to the level of your subject. It's a good rule of thumb that your camera be at eye level of your subject. This is particularly important when photographing children or small animals. If you don't get down to the eye-level of your subject, the image will appear at an improper angle.

Eye contact plays several important roles in photography. When viewing a photograph, people naturally examine the quality of the eyes before looking at the rest of the photo. If the eyes are sharp and in focus, the rest of the photo will be deemed to be the same. Also, the degree of eye contact also can change the "feel" of a photograph. I'm sure at some point you've looked at a photo or painting where it seemed as though the eyes were following you as your moved around the room. This is the result of the subject looking directly at the camera. While your subject doesn't always have to stare directly into the lens, be aware that the degree of eye contact can affect the quality and feel of your photograph.

STEP 5 : COLORING THE SHIRT

Adjusting the color of an object using the Color Balance dialog box is just one way to change colors. For the shirt of the other man in the image, we'll adjust the color using the Hue/Saturation function. This function allows us to adjust the hue levels in an image.

A. Repeat Steps 2 and 3 described earlier to select the shirt of the man on the right. Remember to first click the "New selection" button before you begin, as Photoshop remembers your last selection mode. (In this case, the last mode we used was subtraction.)

B. Click Image | Adjustments | Hue/Saturation. The Hue/Saturation dialog box will open.

C. Click and drag the slider bars to set the following levels: Hue: -3, Saturation: +68, Brightness: -5. The man's shirt should now be a peachy color.

D. Click OK. The dialog box will close.

E. Press Ctrl+D (PC) or Command+D (Mac) to deselect your selection.

F. Press Ctrl+0 (PC) or Command+0 (Mac) to zoom out to full view again.

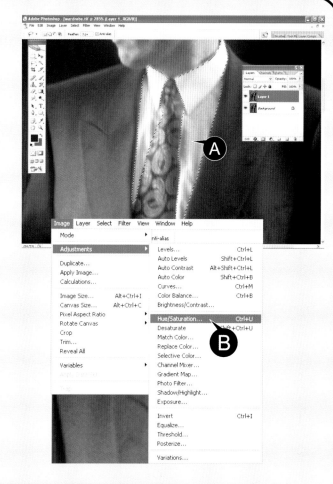

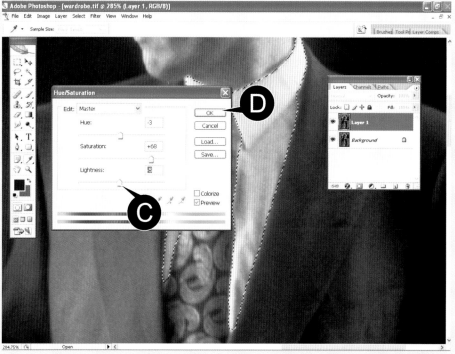

Miracle **Wrinkle** Cream

There is a lyric from a Cher song that goes, "If I could turn back time, if I could find a way...." Well Cher, now you can turn back time using Photoshop. There is a billion dollar industry built around making people look younger. Whether it's surgery, creams, ointments, or masks, people will do just about anything to remove their wrinkles. This project will show you how to get rid of those unsightly lines in minutes without spending a dime. By creatively using the blur technique, we will soften all the lines on this man's face to make him look years younger.

Project Files

The file for this project is called wrinkes.tif and can be found at: www.mimosabooks.com/files

Completion Time

After the files have been downloaded, this project should take approximately ten minutes to fifteen minutes to complete.

Degree of Difficulty

☆☆☆

Project Tools

Eraser Tool

Lasso Tool

Palettes

Ensure the following palettes, which can be accessed from the Window menu, are open for this project:

Tools

Layers

STEP 1 : OPEN THE TUTORIAL

Before we can get any work done, we need to first open the file we'll be using in this project.

A. Press Ctrl+O (PC) or Command+O (Mac) to launch the Open dialog box.

B. Browse to the folder where you saved the tutorial files.

C. Click on the file entitled "wrinkles.tif." It will be highlighted.

D. Click the Open button. The file will open.

E. Click the Maximize button to maximize the size of the window.

F. Press Ctrl+0 (PC) or Command+0 (Mac) to zoom to the entire length and width of the picture.

G. Press Ctrl+J (PC) or Command+J (Mac) to create a duplicate layer of the Background layer to work on.

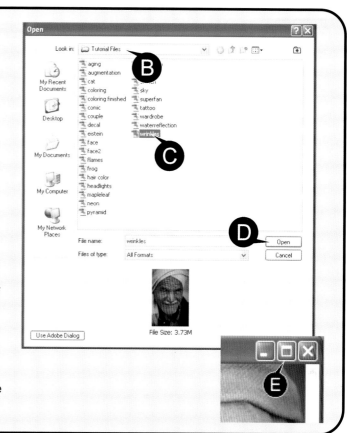

STEP 2 : BLURRING THE WRINKLES

In order to reduce the appearance of wrinkles, we will blur the image using the Gaussian Blur filter. To specify where the blur should be applied, we'll start by creating a selection.

A. Click the Lasso Tool button.

B. Click and drag around the man's face. Don't worry about being extremely accurate, just make sure the entire face is included in the selection. When you release the mouse button, a selection will appear.

C. Click Filter | Blur | Gaussian Blur. The Gaussian Blur dialog box will appear.

D. Click and drag the slider until the Radius amount is 13 pixels.

E. Click OK. The blur will be applied to the face.

F. Press Ctrl+D (PC) or Command+D (Mac) to remove the selection.

STEP 3 : BLENDING THE LAYERS

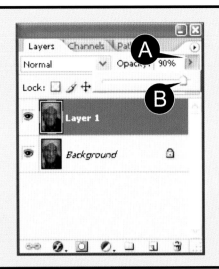

There's no doubt that at this point the man's skin appears much smoother. The only problem is that it just doesn't look realistic. His eyes, mouth, and nose are also blurred, and there are no wrinkles at all. In this step, we'll change the opacity of the layer so that some of the original image, sitting beneath, will show through.

A. Click the Opacity arrow in the Layers palette. A slider bar will appear.

B. Click and drag the slider until it reaches 90%. The Background layer will now show through slightly.

STEP 4 : ADDING THE DETAILS

We still need to focus the details of the man's face, including the eyes, mouth, and nose. To do this, we'll simply erase parts of the blurred layer so that the Background layer will show through.

A. Click the Eraser Tool button.

B. Click the Brush Preset picker to expand the menu.

C. Click and drag the sliders to enter the following settings: Master Diameter: 70px, Hardness: 0%.

D. Enter 50% for both the Opacity and Flow boxes. This will control how much gets erased as you click.

E. Click and drag around the outside edge of the man's face to delete the blurred edges. You may have to drag several times over the area for the background to show through.

F. Click and drag over the man's beard until it shows through.

G. Repeat Step F over the man's eyes, nose, and mouth until they show through.

H. Repeat Step F in a few other random locations to bring some of the background through.

Growing Old
Unnaturally

6

Project Files

The file for this project is called aging.tif and can be found at: www.mimosabooks.com/files

Completion Time

After the files have been downloaded, this project should take approximately fifteen minutes to twenty minutes to complete.

Degree of Difficulty

☆☆☆☆☆

Project Tools

🪣 Paint Bucket Tool
👇 Smudge Tool
🔍 Zoom Tool
🔗 Lasso Tool
🖐 Burn Tool

Palettes

Ensure the following palettes, which can be accessed from the Window menu, are open for this project:

Tools
Navigator
Layers
Colors

To be completely honest with you, there aren't a lot of people demanding a project that will make them look older. That being said, there's no better way to get revenge on an enemy or someone you simply don't like than by aging them. So, whether you want to get back at someone or you want to look into the crystal ball to see what you might look like ten to fifteen years down the line, you can follow the steps of this project. This project uses mostly drawing tools to enhance and lengthen laugh lines and wrinkles. It also uses the Burn tool to create some realistic-looking aging spots.

STEP 1 : OPEN THE TUTORIAL

Before we can get any work done, we need to first open the file we'll be using in this project.

A. Press Ctrl+O (PC) or Command+O (Mac) to launch the Open dialog box.

B. Browse to the folder where you saved the tutorial files.

C. Click on the file entitled "aging.tif." It will be highlighted.

D. Click the Open button. The file will open.

E. Press the Maximize button to maximize the size of the window.

F. Press Ctrl+J (PC) or Command+J (Mac) to create a copy of the Background layer that we will use as our working layer.

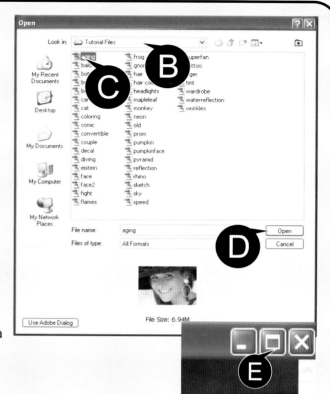

Ready to print the image you've created? If so, you can press Ctrl+P (PC) or Command+P (Mac) to bring up the Print dialog box. Once it is open, you can specify print settings, including: which printer to print to, the number of copies, the quality of the print, etc.

STEP 2 : ACCENTUATING

Although the image is of a relatively young woman, she is smiling, therefore, we can see some of her existing laugh lines and wrinkles. Using the Smudge tool, we are going to increase the length and depth of some of her existing wrinkles.

A. Click the Zoom Tool button.

B. Click and drag around the woman's left eye. As you drag a marquee will appear indicating the area where the zoom will occur.

C. Click the Smudge Tool button. You will now be presented options for the Smudge tool in the options bar.

D. Click the Brush Preset picker arrow. A menu with different options for the brush will appear.

E. Click and drag the sliders to set the following values: Master Diameter: 10px, Hardness: 75%.

F. Repeat Step D to close the menu.

G. Position your mouse pointer at the far left edge of one of her wrinkles.

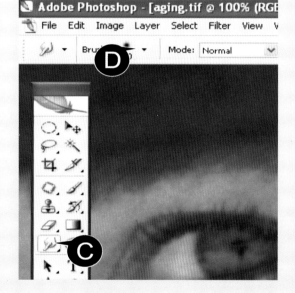

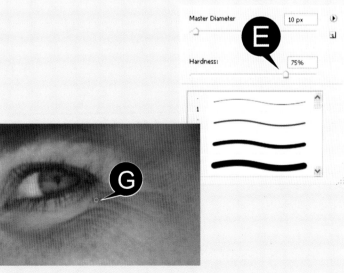

STEP 2 : ACCENTUATING CONT.

H. Click and drag, following the path of the wrinkle, and continue dragging past the end of the existing wrinkle to extend it.

I. Repeat Step H several times on the same wrinkle to thicken and extend the wrinkle.

J. Repeat Steps G - I for the other large wrinkle on the woman's right eye.

K. Press Ctrl+0 (PC) or Command+0 (Mac) to zoom to the entire length and width of the picture.

L. Repeat Steps A - J for the woman's right eye.

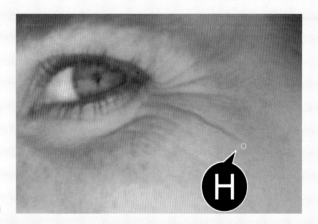

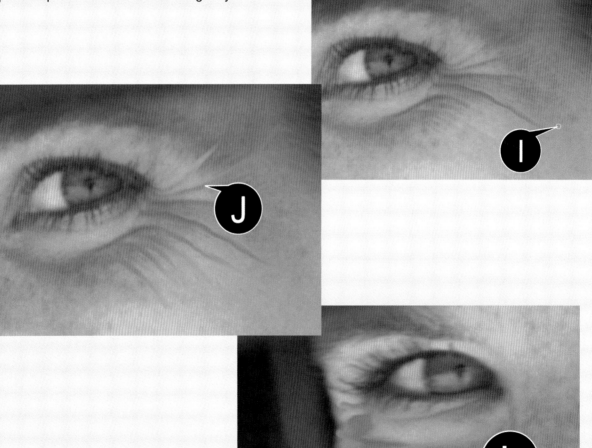

STEP 3 : MOUTH LINES

The lines surrounding the woman's mouth are going to be extended and thickened. We will do this using the same procedure that we followed in the last step with the Smudge tool. The only difference is that we are going to increase the size of the brush.

A. Click the Brush Preset picker arrow. A menu with different options for the brush will appear.

B. Click and drag the sliders to set the following values: Master Diameter: 20px, Hardness: 85%.

C. Position your mouse pointer over the area of the laugh line that is just to the right of the woman's lips.

D. Click and drag downward until you are about halfway down to the woman's chin.

E. Repeat Step D two more times to thicken and extend the line.

F. Repeat Steps C to E for the other side of the woman's mouth.

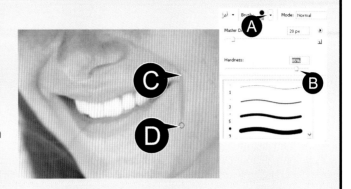

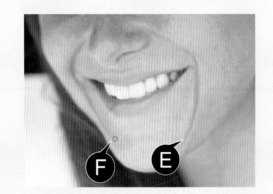

STEP 4 : ADDING WRINKLES

We've accentuated the woman's wrinkles, but to really add a dimension of aging, we will need to add additional wrinkles. We'll do this by using the Burn tool.

A. Click the Zoom Tool button.

B. Click and drag around the woman's left eye. As you drag, a marquee will appear indicating the area where the zoom will occur.

C. Click and hold the Dodge Tool button. A list of options will appear.

D. Click the Burn Tool option. You will now be presented options for the Burn tool in the options bar.

STEP 4 : ADDING WRINKLES CONT.

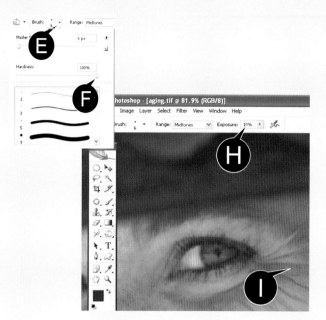

E. Click the Brush Preset picker arrow. A menu with different options for the brush will appear.

F. Click and drag the sliders to set the following values: Master Diameter: 6px, Hardness: 100%.

G. Repeat Step E to close the menu.

H. Enter the following settings into the options bar: Range: Midtones, Exposure: 10%.

I. Click and drag outward, starting from the corner of the woman's eye.

J. Repeat Step I ten more times in slightly different locations around the woman's eye to add more wrinkles.

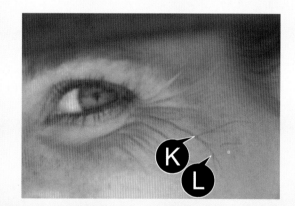

K. Click and drag starting at the halfway point of one wrinkle and branching outward to add a wrinkle to the existing one.

L. Repeat Step K on the other side of the same wrinkle.

M. Repeat Steps I-J with several other wrinkles that surround the right eye.

N. Press Ctrl+0 (PC) or Command+0 (Mac) to zoom to see the entire picture.

O. Repeat the above steps for the woman's right eye, and the area around her mouth and lips. Repeatedly change the size of the wrinkles by adjusting the brush size as described in Steps E - F above. You can also change the exposure level in the options bar to make the wrinkles lighter or darker. The higher the exposure level, the darker the wrinkle will be. Keep in mind that we are going for a subtle change.

STEP 5 : ADDING LIVER SPOTS

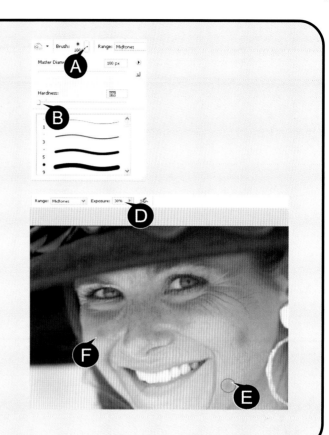

As we get older, some people get blemishes on their faces called liver spots. We'll add the liver spots by using the same tool we used in the last step -- the Burn tool. The only difference is that we will increase the size and the type of brush.

A. Click the Brush Preset picker arrow. A menu with different options for the brush will appear.

B. Click and drag the sliders to set the following values: Master Diameter: 100px, Hardness: 0%.

C. Repeat Step A to close the menu.

D. Enter the following settings into the options bar: Range: Midtones, Exposure: 30%.

E. Click once on the face to create a liver spot.

F. Repeat Step E in a couple of other locations to create more spots on the woman's face.

NOTES

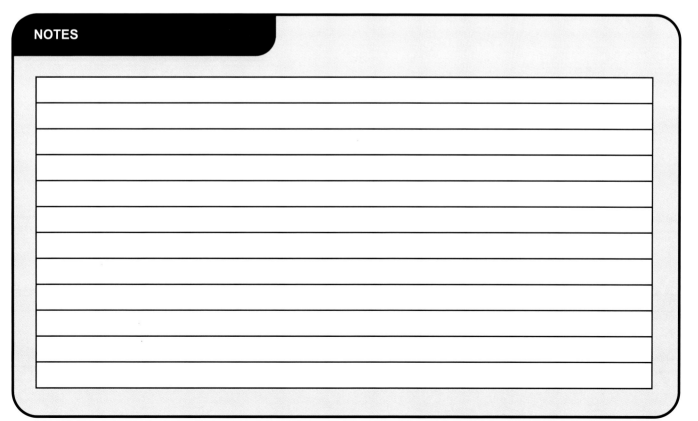

STEP 6 : YELLOWING THE TEETH

Most elderly people don't have shiny, pearly white teeth like our model, unless they've had some extensive dental work done. To change the tone of the woman's teeth, we'll fill a selection with the color yellow on a new layer and then change the opacity of that layer.

A. Click the Zoom Tool button.

B. Click and drag a marquee around the woman's teeth to zoom into that area.

C. Click the Lasso Tool button.

D. Click the "New selection" button in the options bar, if it is not already selected.

E. Enter a "1" in the Feather box.

F. Click on the New layer button in the Layers palette.

G. Click and drag around the woman's teeth to create a selection.

H. Click on a yellowish color in the Colors palette.

I. Click the Paint Bucket Tool button. Make sure that none of the check boxes in the options bar are selected.

J. Click anywhere within the selection. The selection will be filled with a yellow color.

K. Click the Opacity arrow in the Layers palette. This will bring up a slider bar that you can use to adjust the opacity level of the layer.

L. Drag the slider until it reaches 20%

M. Press Ctrl+D (PC) or Command+D (Mac) to remove the selection.

N. Press Ctrl+0 (PC) or Command+0 (Mac) to zoom to the entire length and width of the picture. You've now finished aging the model.

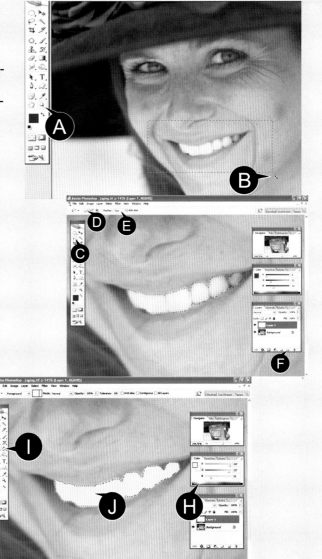

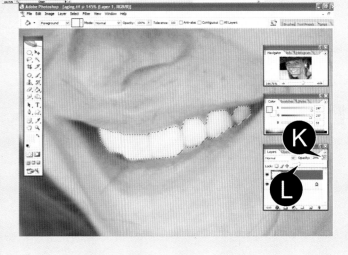

Superfan

Project Files

The files for this project are called mapleleaf.tif and superfan.tif and can be found at:
www.mimosabooks.com/files

Completion Time

After the files have been downloaded, this project should take approximately ten minutes to fifteen minutes to complete.

Degree of Difficulty

Project Tools

	Magic Wand Tool
	Eraser Tool
	Lasso Tool
	Move Tool

Palettes

Ensure the following palettes, which can be accessed from the Window menu, are open for this project:

Tools
Navigator
Layers

There is a classic episode from the hit television show "Seinfeld" in which one of the character's boyfriends paints his face to go to a hockey game and shouts out "You suck, Messier!" Whether you've seen the episode or not, almost anyone who has attended a professional or amateur sporting event has witnessed the "Superfan" -- that person who takes the game and their passion for the team far too seriously. In this project, you can emulate that "Superfan" look with any photo. We'll use a maple leaf image that was downloaded from the Internet as our template for painting on the makeup.

STEP 1 : OPEN THE TUTORIAL

Before we can get any work done, we need to first open the file we'll be using in this project.

A. Press Ctrl+O (PC) or Command+O (Mac) to launch the Open dialog box.

B. Browse to the folder where you saved the tutorial files.

C. Click on the file entitled "superfan.tif." It will be highlighted.

D. Click the Open button. The file will open.

E. Click the Maximize button to expand the window.

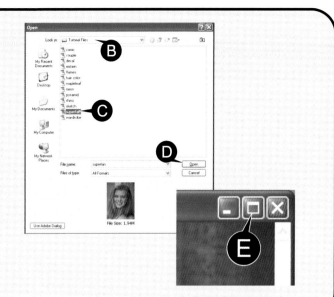

STEP 2 : ISOLATING THE FACE

We only want to apply the superfan makeup to the face of the woman, so we need to isolate that area. Prior to the isolation, we'll duplicate the background layer so that we can pre- vent doing any damage to the original image.

A. Press Ctrl+J (PC) or Command+J (Mac) to duplicate the background layer.

B. Click on the Lasso Tool button. If the Lasso Tool button isn't present (for example, if the Magnetic Lasso Tool button is showing), you may have to click and hold on the button and select the Lasso Tool option.

C. Type "10" in the Feather box in the options bar.

D. Click and drag around the woman's face. Don't worry if your selection isn't perfect, we've feathered the outside of the selection so that it'll look realistic.

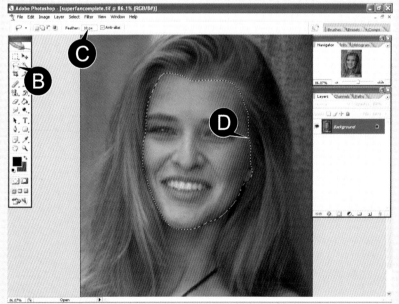

STEP 3 : APPLYING THE MAKEUP

The makeup that we are applying is actually just a change in the color hue of the woman's face. By changing the color hue, we keep the tones and highlights so that the color change looks realistic.

A. Click Image | Adjustments | Hue/Saturation. The Hue/Saturation dialog box will open.

B. Click and drag the sliders to adjust the settings to the following: Hue: +180, Saturation: -18, and Lightness: - 14.

C. Click OK. The setting will be applied.

D. Press Ctrl+D (PC) or Command+D (Mac) to remove the selection.

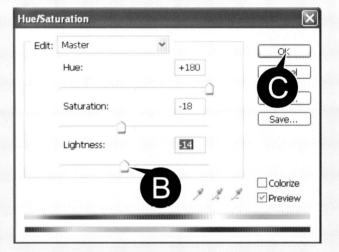

PHOTOGRAPHY 101

Avoid the Jitters - Cameras come in all shapes and sizes, and with the progression of technology, we are seeing smaller and smaller cameras becoming more common. This is particularly true in the case of digital cameras, of which credit size models are now commonplace. One of the problems with these small cameras is that they multiply the shakes in your hands, which can result in blurred images. Regardless of the size of your camera, there are several steps you can take to avoid blurred images. Most importantly, hold your camera with two hands. Typically, you will use your right hand to press the shutter and your left hand to support the camera. Another trick for steadier shots is to tuck your elbows into your body. This added support will ensure that the camera remains steady.

STEP 4 : APPLYING THE LOGO

The logo that we are going to apply was downloaded off the Internet. It is a simple image that we will adjust to fit the proportions of the woman's face.

A. Click File | Place. A dialog box will open from which you can select your file to place.

B. Navigate to the folder that contains your tutorial files.

C. Double-click on the file called "mapleleaf.tif." The Place procedure will begin, and a new layer will be created.

D. Click the Commit button on the options bar. The image will be placed.

E. Click the Opacity drop-down arrow. Click and drag the slider until the opacity level reaches about 20%. This way you'll be able to see the maple leaf, and the image of the woman at the same time.

F. Click the Move Tool button. A series of handles will appear around the maple leaf image.

G. Position your mouse pointer over one of the corner handles. Click and drag inward until the maple leaf is about half the size of the woman's face.

H. Position your mouse pointer over the middle of the maple leaf. Click and drag the image until it is centered on her face.

I. Click the Commit button on the options bar.

J. Click Edit | Transform | Warp. A grid will appear around the maple leaf image. This grid will allow you to warp the image so that it will contour with the woman's face.

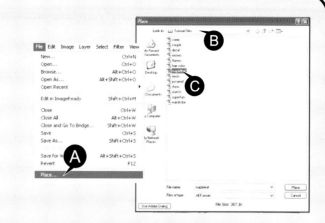

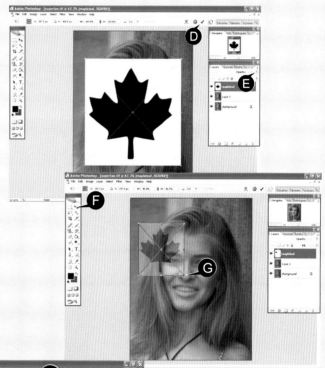

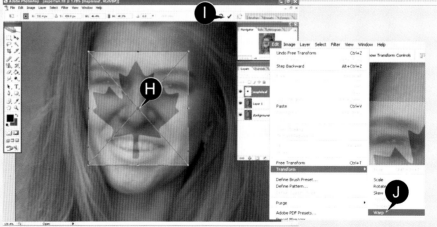

STEP 4 : APPLYING CONT.

K. Click and drag the upper-right middle node down-ward slightly.

L. Repeat Step J with the other three middle nodes.

M. Click the Commit button on the options bar.

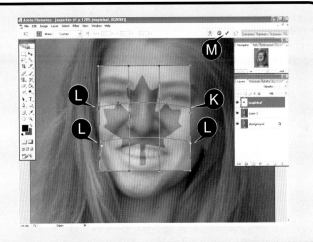

STEP 5 : ISOLATING THE LOGO

In order to fill the logo with color, we are going to create a selection from it. Using the selection, we will copy and paste from the original image and then change the color. Sound confusing? Don't worry -- it's not. Just follow these steps:

A. Click the Magic Wand Tool button.

B. Click once on the darker part of the maple leaf image. In other words, click on the leaf itself, not its surrounding area. A selection will be created, and we can now get rid of the image.

C. Click the Delete layer button in the Layers palette. A dialog box will appear confirming that you would like to delete the layer.

D. Click Yes. The layer will now be gone.

E. Click on the Background layer. It will now be highlighted.

F. Press Ctrl+C (PC) or Command+C (Mac) to copy the image within the selection.

G. Click on Layer 2 in the Layers palette. It will be highlighted.

H. Press Ctrl+V (PC) or Command +V (Mac). The part of the image you copied will be pasted on a new layer. You are now ready to change the color of the leaf.

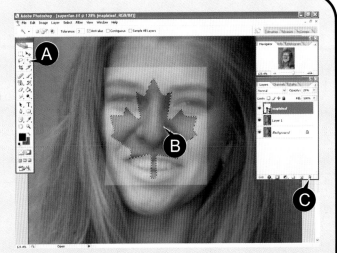

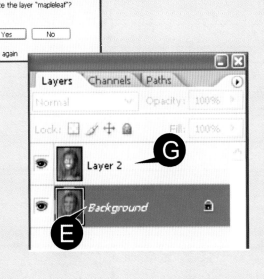

STEP 6 : ADJUSTING LEAF COLORS

To make the leaf appear a whitish color, we will take the same approach that we used earlier and apply a change to the color hue.

A. Click Image | Adjustments | Hue/Saturation. The Hue/Saturation dialog box will open.

B. Click and drag the sliders to adjust the settings to the following: Hue: +0, Saturation: -51, and Lightness: +17.

C. Click OK. The setting will be applied.

D. Click on the Blending Mode arrow to see a list of options.

E. Click Hard Light. The image will now be the right consistency of white.

STEP 7 : MERGING LAYERS

Before we tidy up our image, we are going to combine all of the layers we created. This will make our editing in the next step easier.

A. Hold down the Shift key and click on Layer 1. Both Layer 1 and Layer 2 should now be highlighted.

B. Click Layer | Merge Layers. The two selected layers will now be merged together.

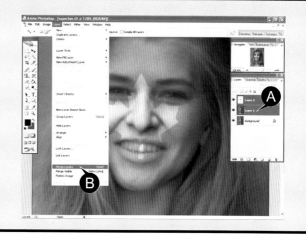

STEP 8 : TIDYING UP

Even superfans know where to draw the line, and most don't apply face paint to their eyeballs, teeth, and lips. In this step, we'll use the Eraser tool to remove some areas that are covered by the make-up we applied. Because we created a copy of the original image when we started this project, as we erase parts of the layer with the makeup, the original image will show through.

A. Click the Eraser Tool button.

B. Click on the Brush Preset picker arrow. A menu will appear where you can adjust the setting for the Eraser tool.

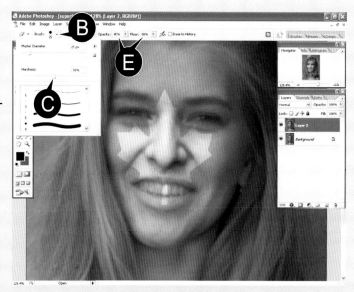

C. Click and drag the sliders to adjust the following settings: Master Diameter: 25px, and Hardness: 50%.

D. Repeat Step B to close the menu.

E. Type 45% in the Opacity box and 50% in the flow box.

F. Click and drag the Zoom slider in the Navigator palette to about 191% to zoom into the woman's face.

G. Click and drag over her lips, teeth, eyes, and eyebrows to remove the makeup in those areas.

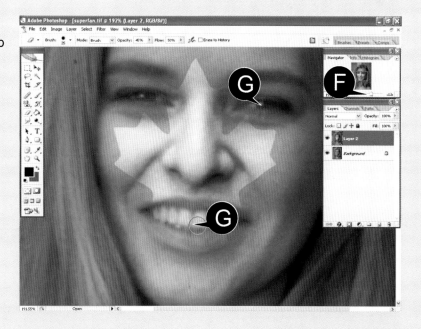

Trading Faces

8

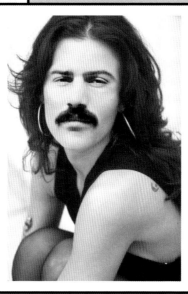

As disturbing as the above images are, this is one of my favorite projects. The question I probably get most often when I teach people Photoshop is, "How can I put my face on someone else's body?" Well, you'll find the answer to this question in this project. The key to switching faces lies in matching the skin tones. To accomplish this, we'll adjust the hue levels and the brightness of the skin. After that, we'll adjust the opacity of the layers to help them blend with one another. Once you get the hang of this technique, you'll be switching faces of all of the members of your family, friends, and coworkers.

Project Files

The files for this project are called face.tif and face2.tif. They can be found at: www.mimosabooks.com/files

Completion Time

After the files have been downloaded, this project should take approximately ten minutes to twenty minutes to complete.

Degree of Difficulty

☆☆☆☆☆

Project Tools

🔍 Zoom Tool

✏️ Eraser Tool

🔾 Lasso Tool

⬥ Move Tool

Palettes

Ensure the following palettes, which can be accessed from the Window menu, are open for this project:

Tools

STEP 1 : OPEN THE TUTORIAL

Before we can get any work done, we need to first open the files we'll be using in this project.

A. Press Ctrl+O (PC) or Command+O (Mac) to launch the Open dialog box.

B. Browse to the folder where you saved the tutorial files.

C. Click on the file entitled "face2.tif." It will be high-lighted.

D. Hold down the Ctrl key (PC) or Command key (Mac) and click on the file "face.tif." This file will also be highlighted.

E. Click the Open button. The files will open.

F. Click the Maximize button. The window will expand to fill the screen.

G. Click the Zoom tool.

H. Click and drag around the man's face to zoom into that area.

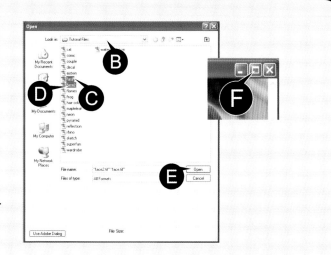

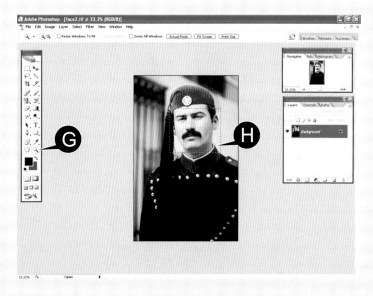

Photoshop CS and CS2 users have the ability to create their own keyboard shortcuts. You can access a dialog box that will allow you to customize your keyboard shortcuts by selecting Keyboard Shortcuts from the Edit menu.

STEP 2 : SELECTING THE FACE

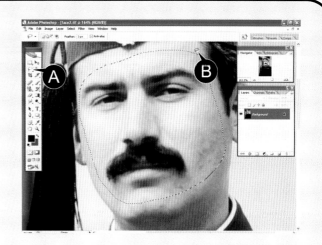

To bring the man's face to the image of the woman, we'll start by making a selection and then copying and pasting to the other image.

A. Click the Lasso Tool.

B. Click and drag around the man's face. Include only the area that surrounds his eyes, nose, and mouth. When you release the mouse button, a marquee will appear around the area you selected.

C. Press Ctrl+C (PC) or Command+C (Mac) to copy the selection.

D. Click Window | face.tif. The image of the woman will appear.

E. Click the Maximize button to enlarge the window.

F. Click the Zoom Tool button.

G. Click and drag around the woman's face to zoom into that area.

H. Press Ctrl+V (PC) or Command+V (Mac) to paste the man's face. It will appear on a separate layer.

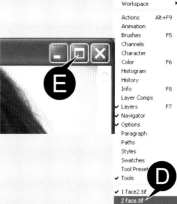

STEP 3 : ADJUSTING THE FACE

We'll have to enlarge and rotate the man's face so that it appears to be the same size as the woman's face. We'll do this using the Move tool.

A. Click the Move Tool button. A series of handles will appear around the man's face.

B. Position the mouse pointer over the top left handle. Click and drag outward to increase the size of the face. Enlarge the selection until it is about the same size of the woman's face.

C. Position the mouse pointer just outside the bottom right handle. You'll know you are in the right place when the mouse pointer turns into a curved double-sided arrow.

D. Click and drag downward slightly to rotate the face until it's in line with the current image.

E. Position the mouse pointer over the middle of the man's face. Click and drag it until it is centered over the woman's face.

F. Click the Commit button in the options bar.

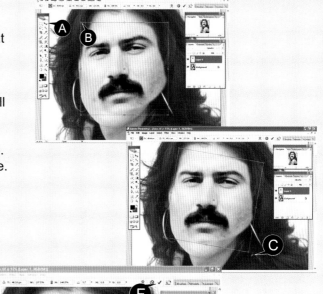

STEP 4 : ADJUSTING COLORS

The shades of the man's face don't quite match the shades of the woman's face. We'll adjust the colors by manipulating the hue, brightness, and contrast levels.

A. Click Image | Adjustments | Hue/Saturation. The Hue/Saturation dialog box will open.

B. Click and drag the Saturation slider until it reaches 20.

C. Click the OK button.

D. Click Image | Adjustments | Brightness/Contrast. The Brightness/Contrast dialog box will open.

E. Click and drag the Brightness slider to 10.

F. Click OK. The brightness adjustments will take effect.

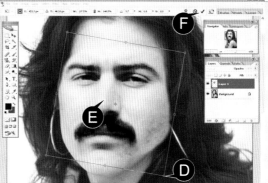

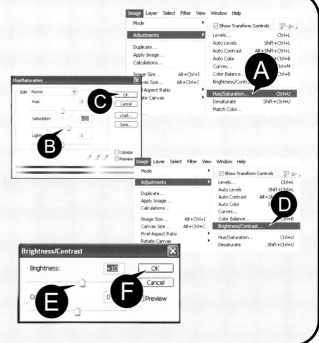

STEP 5 : CLEANING THE IMAGE

As it stands now, the image still looks quite fake. To fix this, we are going to blend the man's face with the woman's face. Although Photoshop gives us a variety of different methods for blending, we'll simply make a copy of the Background layer and use the Eraser tool.

A. Click on the Background layer. It will be highlighted.

B. Press Ctrl+J (PC) or Command+J (Mac) to duplicate the layer.

C. Position the mouse pointer over the Background Copy layer. When the mouse pointer turns into a small hand, you are in the right place.

D. Click and drag upward until a dark line appears above Layer 1.

E. Release the mouse button. You will now see only the image of the woman on the screen. We are going to erase parts of the face so that we can see the man's face underneath.

F. Click the Eraser Tool button.

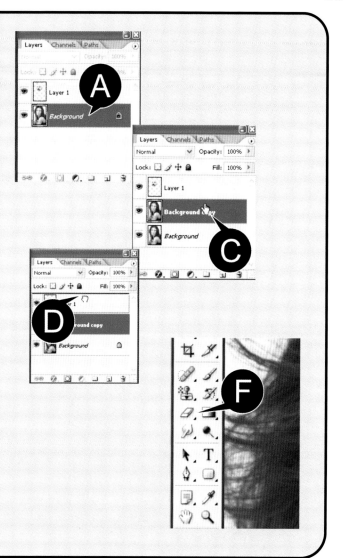

You can use a keyboard shortcut to quickly open the Hue/Saturation dialog box. Pressing Ctrl + U (PC) or Command + U (Mac) will launch the dialog box so that you can quickly make adjustments to your color levels.

STEP 5 : CLEANING CONT.

G. Click the Brush Preset picker to expand the menu.

H. Click and drag the sliders to these levels: Master Diameter: 95px and Hardness: 0%.

I. Repeat Step G to close the menu.

J. Type 50% for the Opacity in the options bar.

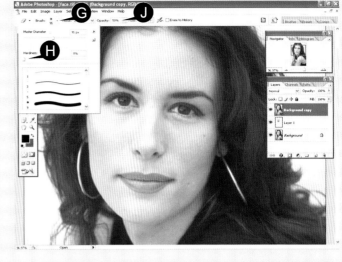

K. Click and drag on the woman's eyes, nose, and mouth areas. As you drag, she will begin to disappear, and the man's face will begin to appear.

L. Repeat Step K until the man's face is showing through.

M. Click and drag the Zoom slider in the Navigator palette to about 40% to view the results.

Tinted Windows

9

There's a line from a famous hip hop song by a group called Run-DMC that goes "tinted windows don't mean nothin', we know who's inside." If you think contrary to the band and like the idea of tinting your windows, you can do so virtually in Photoshop. When you get your windows tinted in real life, you have to make a commitment to the level of tint that you want. This isn't the case in Photoshop, because you can adjust the brightness and contrast levels to get the tint level that you would like. This project will teach you some of the basics of making and adjusting selections.

Project Files

The file for this project is called tint.tif and can be found at:
www.mimosabooks.com/files

Completion Time

After the files have been downloaded, this project should take approximately five minutes to ten minutes to complete.

Degree of Difficulty

Project Tools

 Magnetic Lasso Tool

Palettes

Ensure the following palettes, which can be accessed from the Window menu, are open for this project:

Tools

STEP 1 : OPEN THE TUTORIAL

Before we can get any work done, we need to first open the files we'll need for this project.

A. Press Ctrl+O (PC) or Command+O (Mac) to launch the Open dialog box.

B. Browse to the folder where you saved the tutorial files.

C. Click on the file entitled "tint.tif." It will be highlighted.

D. Click the Open button. The file will open.

E. Click the Maximize button to enlarge the window.

F. Press Ctrl+0 (PC) or Command+0 (Mac) to zoom to full view.

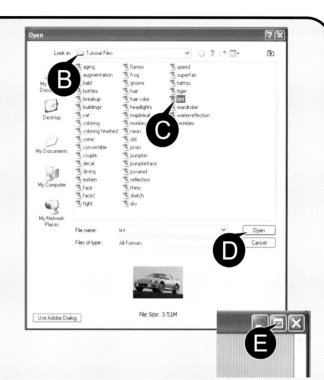

STEP 2 : ISOLATING THE WINDOWS

Our goal is to isolate the windows so that we can darken them without affecting the rest of the image. To do this, we are going to make use of the Magnetic Lasso tool.

A. Click and hold the Lasso Tool button. A list of different selection tools will appear.

B. Click the Magnetic Lasso Tool option.

C. Enter "1" in the Feather box.

D. Click and drag around the outside edge of the windshield. As you drag, a line with little nodes on it will appear, previewing the location of your selection. You can also click in certain points around the outside of the windshield to anchor the nodes.

E. Double-click once your line reaches the point where you started. A selection marquee will now appear around the windshield.

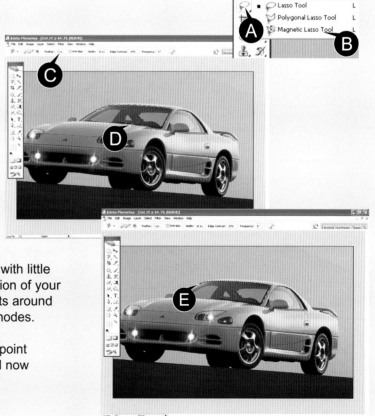

STEP 3 : SELECTING THE OTHER WINDOW

Rather than tinting one window at a time, we are going to apply the tint all at one time. To do this, we'll need to ensure that both windows are selected. Using the "Add to selection" option, we can have multiple areas selected at the same time.

A. Click the "Add to selection" button in the options bar. This will allow you to add areas to your selection.

B. Click and drag around the driver's side window. When you release the mouse button, that area will be selected along with the windshield.

STEP 4 : TINTING THE WINDOWS

The process of tinting windows is simply a matter of changing the brightness levels.

A. Click Image | Adjustments | Brightness/Contrast. The Brightness/Contrast dialog box will open.

B. Click and drag the sliders to enter the following settings: Brightness: -90, Contrast: -15.

C. Click OK. The settings will take effect.

D. Press Ctrl+D (PC) or Command+D (Mac) to remove the selection. Just like that you've tinted the windows!

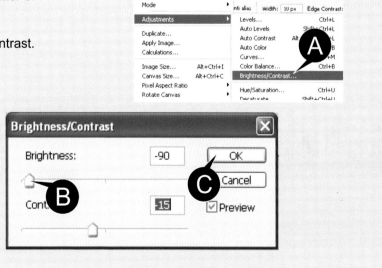

Turn On Your
Headlights

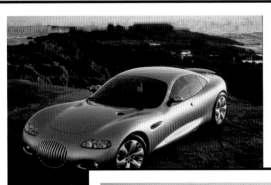

Several years ago, laws were passed in almost every state requiring that all new cars must have daytime running lights. Ultimately, having your lights on all the time is simply a safer way to drive. If you happen to have an older model car, don't worry. You can create the illusion of illuminated lights by using Photoshop. Not only will we turn on the main highlights, we will also add a yellow glow to the fog lamps of this vehicle. We'll be using two different techniques for adding light to this vehicle. For the headlamps, we are going to apply a Lens Flare filter, and for the fog lamps we are going to simply adjust the color and change the brightness levels.

Project Files

The file for this project is called headlights.tif and can be found at:
www.mimosabooks.com/files

Completion Time

After the files have been downloaded, this project should take approximately five minutes to ten minutes to complete.

Degree of Difficulty

Project Tools

 Zoom Tool

 Dodge Tool

 Lasso Tool

Palettes

Ensure the following palettes, which can be accessed from the Window menu, are open for this project:

Tools

Layers

STEP 1 : OPEN THE TUTORIAL

Before we can get any work done, we need to first open the file we'll be using for this project.

A. Press Ctrl+O (PC) or Command+O (Mac) to launch the Open dialog box.

B. Browse to the folder where you saved the tutorial files.

C. Click on the file entitled "headlights.tif." It will be highlighted.

D. Click the Open button. The file will open.

E. Click the Maximize button to expand the window to fit the screen.

F. Press Ctrl+0 (PC) or Command+0 (Mac) to fit the image to the screen.

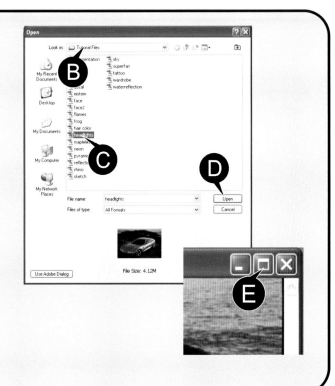

STEP 2 : TURNING ON THE LIGHTS

To turn on the headlights, we'll be using the Lens Flare filter. We simply need to tell the filter which type of lens flare we want and where we want to apply it.

A. Press Ctrl+J (PC) or Command+J (Mac) to create a duplicate of the Background layer on which we will work.

B. Click Filter | Render | Lens Flare. The Lens Flare dialog box will open.

C. Click on the right headlight in the preview window. The cross-hair in the preview window will be over the right headlight.

D. Click and drag the Brightness slider to 40%.

E. Click the radio button beside the 105mm Prime.

F. Click OK. The lens flare will be added to the right headlight.

G. Repeat Steps B - F for the left headlight.

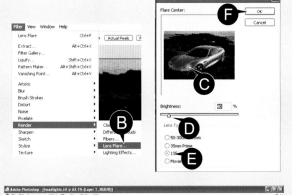

STEP 3 : BRIGHTENING

To turn on the fog lamps, we'll use a different approach than we previously used to turn on the headlights. In this method, we'll start by giving the lamps a yellowish hue, and then in the next step, we'll brighten them.

A. Click on Layer 1 in the Layers palette. It will appear highlighted.

B. Click the Zoom Tool button.

C. Click and drag around the right fog light to zoom into that area.

D. Click on the Lasso Tool button.

E. Click and drag around the fog lamp to create a selection. When you release the mouse button a series of "marching ants" will appear around the selection.

F. Press Ctrl+J (PC) or Command+J (Mac) to create a layer from the selection.

G. Click Image | Adjustments | Hue/Saturation. The Hue/Saturation dialog box will appear.

H. Click and drag the sliders to enter the following settings: Hue: 13, Saturation: 30, Lightness: 0.

I. Click OK. The fog lamp will now have a yellowish tint.

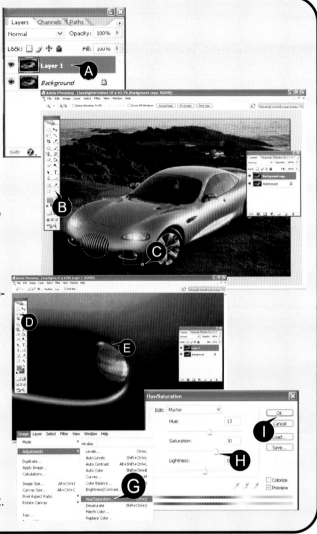

STEP 4 : GLOWING

To make the fog lamps glow slightly, we have a variety of options. In this case, we'll use the Brightness/Contrast feature to make the lamps look a little brighter.

A. Click Image | Adjustments | Brightness/Contrast. The Brightness/Contrast dialog box will open.

B. Click and drag the sliders to enter the following values: Brightness: +40, Contrast: +40.

C. Click OK. The fog lamp will now be much brighter.

D. Press Ctrl+0 (PC) or Command+0 (Mac) to zoom out.

E. Repeat all of Steps 3 and 4 for the other fog lamp.

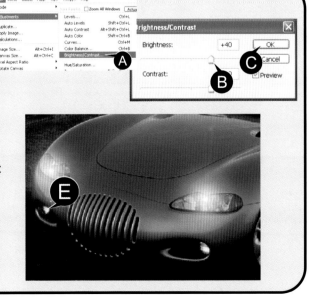

Car Chameleon

There are dozens of auto body shops that will paint your car for you, but how many will guarantee that they'll have your car back to you in 5 minutes? How can you change the color of an object in Photoshop? Let me count the ways. In this project, we'll be using the Replace Color feature to change the color of the car. The Replace Color command simply allows you to pick a specific color to use as a replacement for an existing color. After you've finished coloring the car, you'll tidy up the selection by using the Eraser tool.

Project Files

The file for this project is called car paint.tif and can be found at: www.mimosabooks.com/files

Completion Time

After the files have been downloaded, this project should take approximately ten minutes to fifteen minutes to complete.

Degree of Difficulty

☆☆☆

Project Tools

🔍 Zoom Tool

Magnetic Lasso Tool

Lasso Tool

Palettes

Ensure the following palettes, which can be accessed from the Window menu, are open for this project:

Tools

Navigator

STEP 1 : OPEN THE TUTORIAL

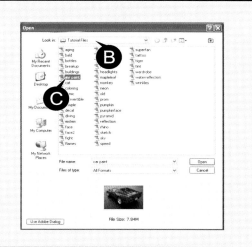

Before we can get any work done, we need to first open a file that we can work with.

A. Press Ctrl+O (PC) or Command+O (Mac) to launch the Open dialog box.

B. Browse to the folder on your computer that contains the tutorial files.

C. Double-click on the file entitled "car paint.tif." The file will open in Photoshop.

STEP 2 : PREPARATION

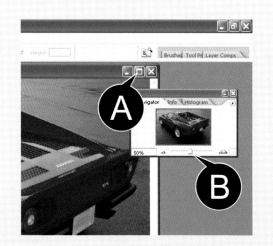

We'll need a close-up view of our car so that we can make sure that our paint job looks just right. To do this, we'll maximize the screen to ensure that the car takes up most of the work area. We'll also create a copy of the background as our work layer.

A. Click the Maximize button.

B. Click the slider in the Navigator until the car takes up most of the screen. Here we will drag until the zoom level is about 64%.

C. Click Layer | Duplicate Layer. A dialog box will open, confirming the creation of the new layer.

D. Click OK. A duplicate of the Background layer will appear. We'll use this as our working layer.

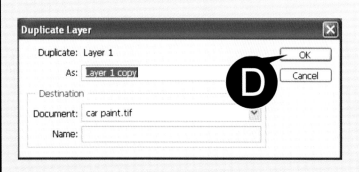

STEP 3 : REPLACE COLORS

Now the fun part -- we are going to replace the colors in our car with a different one. There are probably as many ways to change the color of an object in Photoshop as there are models of cars. (Well, maybe not that many.) Here, we'll use the Replace Colors command to achieve our new paint job.

A. Click Image | Adjustments | Replace Color. The Replace Color dialog box will appear.

B. Click the Fuzziness slider all the way to the right until it reaches the 200 level.

C. Click the Eyedropper Tool button if it is not already selected.

D. Click on the car door just above the black stripe.

E. Set the following values in the dialog box by clicking and dragging on the designated sliders: Hue: -140, Saturation: -18, Brightness: -23.

F. Click OK. The dialog box will close, and the car will be predominately blue.

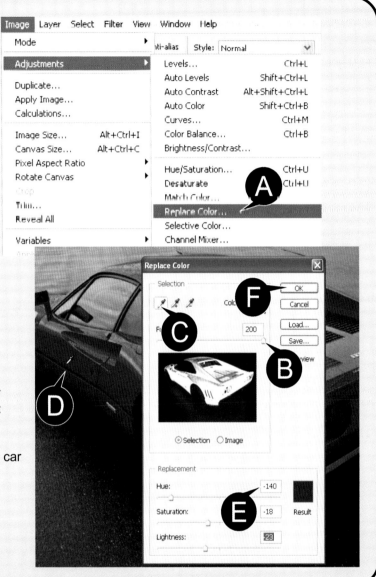

Is your copy of Photoshop up to date? You can always check for updates by clicking on the Help menu and selecting the Updates option.

STEP 4 : TIDYING UP

You'll notice that the brake lights of the car are now also blue. Because we created the coloring on a separate layer, we can simply erase the color over the headlights, and the original brake lights will show through.

A. Select the Zoom tool from the Tools palette.

B. Click and drag a marquee around the brake lights. You'll now have a close-up view of the lights.

C. Click the Eraser Tool button.

D. Click the Brush Preset picker.

E. Click on the Soft 27 Eraser brush.

F. Click carefully around the areas over the brake lights. You will see the brake lights shine through. That's it, you're done. A shiny, new paint job for your car in minutes!

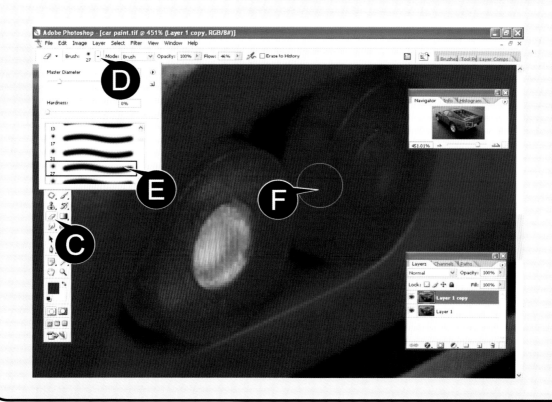

Auto Detailing

12

Project Files

The files for this project are called flames.tif and decal.tif and can be found at: www.mimosabooks.com/files

Completion Time

After the files have been downloaded, this project should take approximately ten minutes to twenty minutes to complete.

Degree of Difficulty

Project Tools

 Eraser Tool

 Move Tool

Magic Wand Tool

Palettes

Ensure the following palettes, which can be accessed from the Window menu, are open for this project:

Tools

Navigator

Layers

Do you remember back in school when you would use a stencil to paint numbers and letters onto paper? We'll be using the same type of approach when applying the flames decal to our car in this project. We basically create a stencil out of an image of flames that was downloaded from the Internet. From there, we will fill the stencil with a color and modify it slightly so that it fits onto our car. This project is surprisingly easy and has some fantastic results. The real beauty of this project is that you can use the same steps described to apply other types of decals to an image of your car. Once you've mastered the steps, try downloading other decals to create different patterns on your photos.

STEP 1 : OPEN THE TUTORIAL

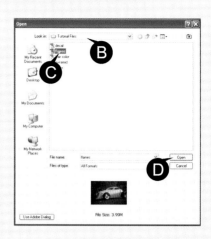

Before we can get any work done, we need to first open the file that we'll need for this project. We'll be opening the picture of the car to which we'll be applying the flames decal.

A. Press Ctrl+O (PC) or Command+O (Mac) to launch the Open dialog box.

B. Browse to the folder where you saved the tutorial files.

C. Click on the file entitled "flames.tif." It will be highlighted.

D. Click the Open button. The file will open.

E. Click the Maximize button to have the window expand to the entire screen.

F. Click and drag the Zoom slider in the Navigator palette to approximately 105% to zoom into the car.

G. Hold down the Space bar. Click and drag to the left. While the space bar is held down, the mouse pointer will change to a hand. As you drag the image will pan. Pan until the entire door of the vehicle is visible. This is where we will be placing the flames decal.

STEP 2 : IMPORTING THE DECAL

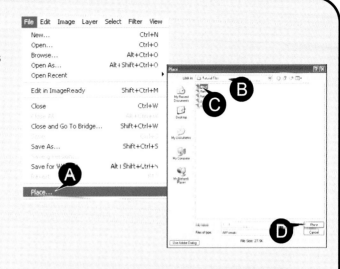

The decal for this project is simply an image that was found while surfing the Internet. The resolution (picture quality) of this image is quite low; but that does not make a difference to us, because we'll simply be using this file to create a selection. After the decal is imported, we'll need to adjust it slightly to fit the proportions of the car.

A Click File | Place. A dialog box will appear.

B. Browse to the folder where you saved the tutorial files.

C. Click on the file called "decal.tif." It will be highlighted.

D. Click the Place button. The file will be imported into your current project.

E. Click the Commit button on the options bar. The decal is now on a separate layer in your image.

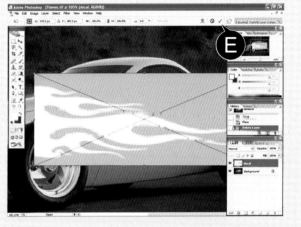

PHOTOGRAPHY 101

Fill 'Er Up - When looking through a viewfinder people sometimes forget that the final size of their picture will typically be 4 x 6. What appears large through the viewfinder may not appear as big when you look at it in its final form. Through the viewfinder, it's easy to over-exaggerate the size of your subject, which can result in a lot of wasted space in your final image. The goal should be having the subject take up as much room as possible within the photo and minimizing the amount of background that appears. The best way to accomplish this is to line up your subject as you normally would and then simply take a couple of steps forward.

STEP 3 : POSITIONING THE DECAL

As you can see, the decal needs to be rotated slightly and repositioned to fit in line with the car door. We'll first make the decal partially transparent so that we can see the car image underneath as we modify the decal. We'll then use the Free Transform option to rotate and adjust the position of the decal.

A. Click the arrow beside the Opacity option. A slider will appear.

B. Click and drag the slider to approximately 60%. This will allow you to see the car underneath while still having the ability to view the decal. You may have to close or reposition some palettes in order to see the entire decal.

C. Click the Move Tool button, if it is not already selected.

D. Click and drag the decal so that it partially over-laps the front tire.

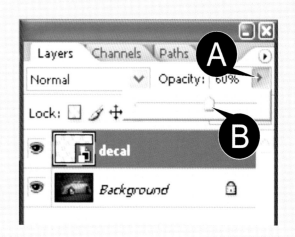

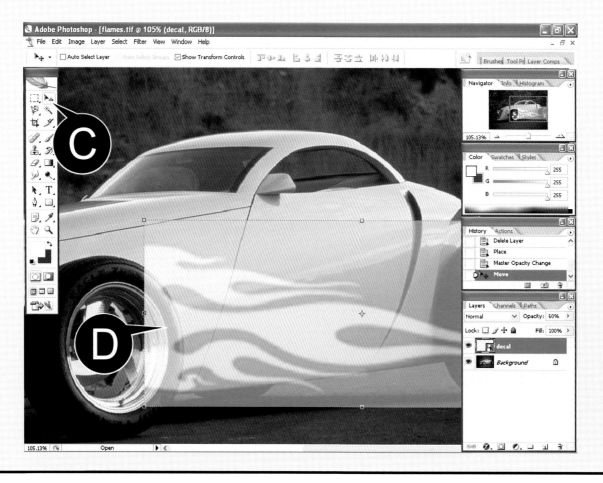

STEP 3 : POSITIONING THE DECAL CONT.

E. Click and drag the Zoom slider in the Navigator palette to approximately 40% to zoom out of the car. This will allow us to see the entire decal.

F. Press Ctrl+T (PC) or Command+T (Mac) to move into Free Transform mode, which will allow you, amongst other things, to rotate the decal.

G. Position the mouse pointer to the right of the middle right node. The mouse pointer will turn into a curved, double-sided arrow.

H. Click and drag upward slightly to rotate the decal. The decal should now flow in line with the car. You can position your mouse pointer over the middle of the decal, and click and drag it, if it needs to be slightly moved.

I. Click the Commit button on the options bar.

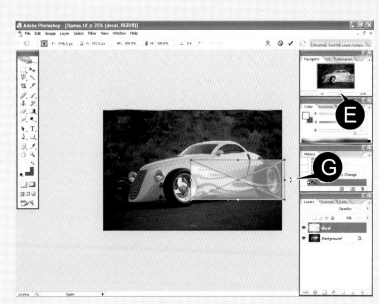

STEP 4 : CREATING A SELECTION

Now that we have the decal in place, we are going to create a selection, which we will later fill with the color of our choice. The Magic Wand tool makes the process of creating a selection as easy as clicking once with the mouse.

A. Click the Magic Wand Tool button.

B. Click once in the flames area of the decal. A series of lines called "marching ants" will appear within the decal, indicating the area of our selection.

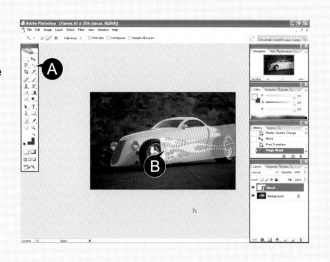

STEP 5 : LAYERS

Once we have a selection created in the shape of the flames decal, we no longer need the original decal. In this step, we will not only delete the existing decal, but we'll also create a new layer on which we will paint the flames. Even though we are deleting the layer where the selection was created, the selection itself will remain.

A. Click the Delete Layer button in the Layers palette. The decal layer will be removed, but the selection will remain.

B. Click Yes if a dialog box appears.

C. Click the New Layer button. A new layer will be created where we will paint our flames.

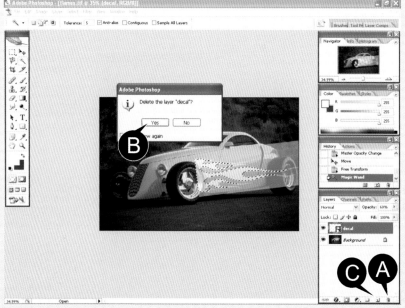

STEP 6 : COLORING THE FLAMES

Photoshop provides you with a myriad of ways to fill or paint an area in your projects. In this step, we'll use the basic Fill command, which fills a selection or an entire layer (if there is no selection made) with a color that you specify. Because we have a selection created, any fill that we select will only be applied to the area within the selection.

A. Click Edit | Fill. The Fill dialog box will appear.

B. Click the Use drop-down button. A menu will appear.

C. Click Color. The Color Picker dialog box will open.

D. Click the desired Hue Range and then click on a desired color.

E. Click the OK button to return to the previous dialog box.

F. Click OK to close the dialog box. The color that you chose will now appear in your selection.

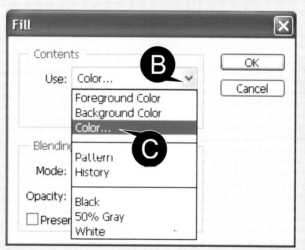

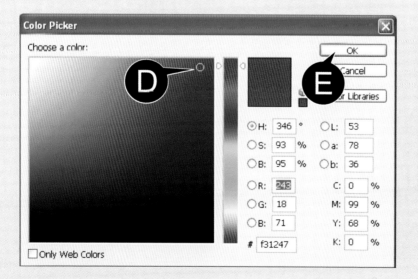

STEP 7 : BLENDING THE FLAMES

At this point, our flames don't look too realistic for several reasons. The first is that they overlap the tires, which is a problem that will be taken care of in the next step. The next problem is that none of the highlights that appear in the car are reflected in the flames. This problem can be resolved by making the flames slightly opaque. Finally, you'll notice that certain parts of the car (especially the small areas in black) are covered by the flames. We can take care of this by blending the flames with the car image itself. Before we start blending, we'll remove those annoying "marching ants" since our selection is no longer needed.

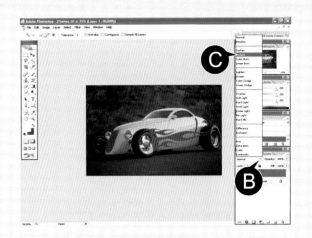

A. Press Ctrl+D (PC) or Command+D (Mac) to remove the selection.

B. Click on the Blending Mode drop-down arrow. A menu of different blending options will appear.

C. Click Multiply. The flames will be blended with the car based on the settings for the Multiply function.

D. Click on the Opacity arrow. A slider bar will appear that will allow you to adjust the opacity.

E. Click and drag the slider until it reaches 64%.

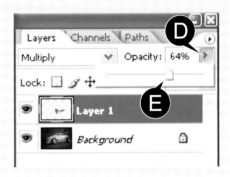

You can learn more about the function of each of the different blend modes by consulting the help files within Photoshop. There you will find a detailed description of each blend mode, what it does, and how it can affect your image. You can access the help files by pressing the F1 key on your keyboard (PC) or clicking Help from the menu bar.

STEP 8 : TIDYING UP

The last thing we need to do in order to complete the project is tidy up the areas of the decal that were overlapping the wheels of the car. To do this, we'll first zoom into the area around the wheels and then we'll erase the excess using the Eraser tool.

A. Click the Zoom Tool button.

B. Click and drag a marquee around the tire area. You will zoom into that area.

C. Click the Eraser Tool button.

D. Click the Brush Preset picker to expand a menu where you can set the properties for the Eraser brush.

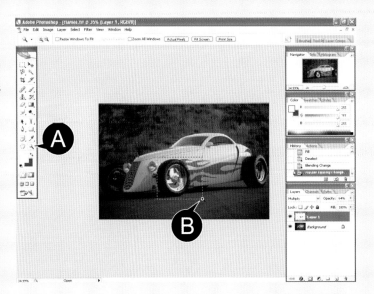

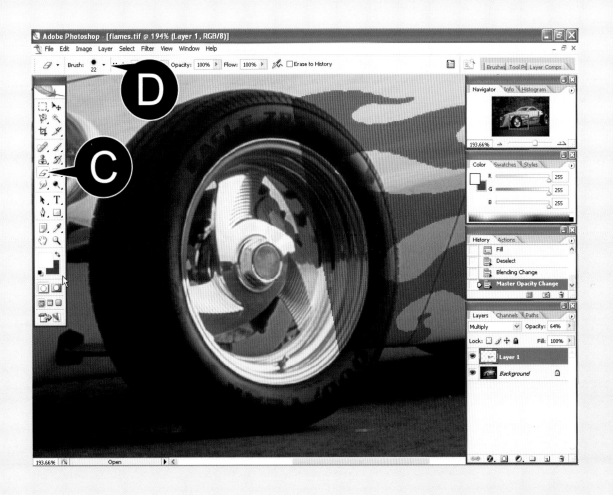

STEP 8 : TIDYING UP CONT.

E. Adjust the Master Diameter slider to approximately 22px.

F. Adjust the Hardness to approximately 50%.

G. Repeat Step D to close the menu.

H. Click and drag over the areas of the decal that overlap the tire. As you drag, they will be erased. If at any point you make a mistake and inadvertently erase an area, press Ctrl+Z (PC) or Command+Z (Mac) to undo your last action.

I. Repeat Steps A - H for the rear tire.

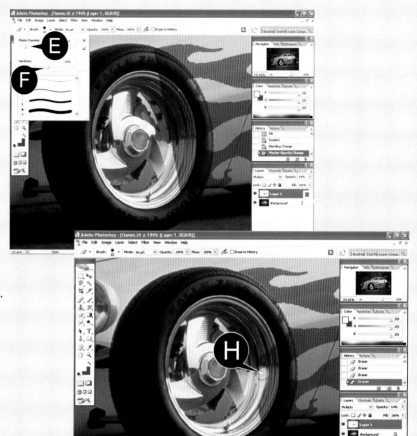

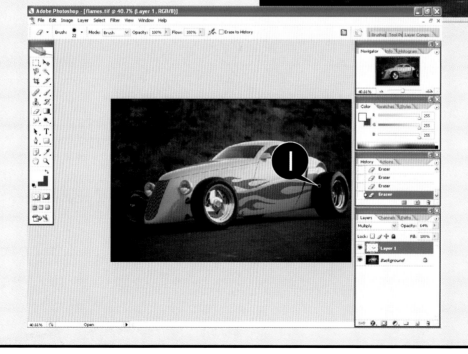

Convertible
Conversion

Have you always dreamed of having a convertible? I've had one; and trust me – they are not all they are cracked up to be. Where I live, there are only three months of the year during which you could actually have the top down. Of those three months, there are only a handful of days when it wouldn't be too scorchingly hot to drive topless. What's the solution? Create a virtual convertible in Photoshop with no large body shop bill involved. With a little help from the Clone Stamp tool, you'll be able to replicate the background after you've removed the roof.

Project Files

The file for this project is called convertible.tif and can be found at:
www.mimosabooks.com/files

Completion Time

After the files have been downloaded, this project should take approximately ten minutes to fifteen minutes to complete.

Degree of Difficulty

Project Tools

Zoom Tool

Clone Stamp Tool

Lasso Tool

Polygon Lasso Tool

Palettes

Ensure the following palettes, which can be accessed from the Window menu, are open for this project:

Tools

STEP 1 : OPEN THE TUTORIAL

Before we can get any work done, we need to first open the file we'll be using in this project.

A. Press Ctrl+O (PC) or Command+O (Mac) to launch the Open dialog box.

B. Browse to the folder where you saved the tutorial files.

C. Click on the file entitled "convertible.tif." It will be highlighted.

D. Click the Open button. The file will open.

E. Click the Maximize button to expand the window to its full size.

F. Press Ctrl+J (PC) or Command+J (Mac) to create a working layer.

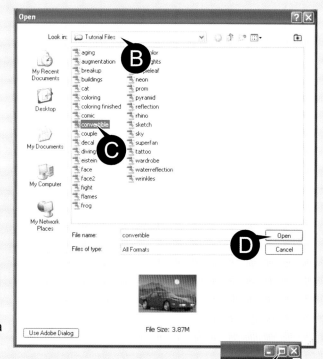

NOTES

STEP 2 : REMOVING THE ROOF

To remove the roof of the car, we'll create a selection that includes the roof, but does not include the interior of the car. To do this, we'll make use of the Polygon Lasso tool which allows us to create straight lines for our selection.

A. Click the Zoom Tool button

B. Click and drag around the roof of the car to zoom into that area.

C. Click and hold the Lasso Tool button. A list of tools will appear.

D. Click the Polygon Lasso Tool option.

E. Enter "0" in the Feather box in the options bar.

F. Click once at the top right corner of the windshield to start the selection.

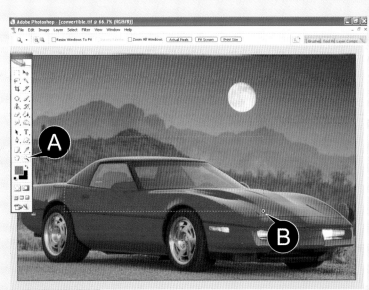

STEP 2 : REMOVING THE ROOF CONT.

G. Click again at the top left corner of the windshield. You will now see a line going across the windshield.

H. Click at the other anchor points as seen in the accompanying figure. We want to include the passenger seat and part of the background behind the roof.

I. Double-click when you reach the starting point of the selection. A marquee line will now appear showing you the selected area.

J. Press Ctrl+0 (PC) or Command+0 (Mac) to zoom to full view.

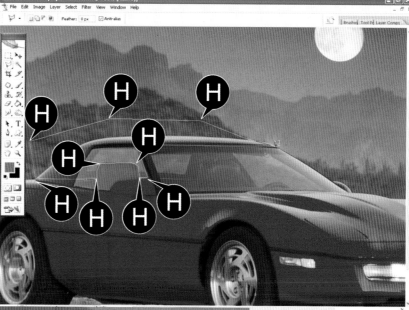

STEP 3 : CLONING

We aren't actually going to remove the roof, but clone some of the background over our selection to hide the roof.

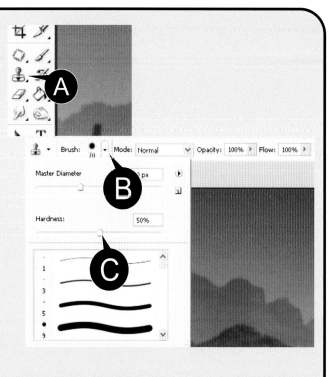

A. Click the Clone Stamp Tool button.

B. Click the Brush Preset picker arrow on the options bar.

C. Click and drag the sliders to enter the following settings: Master Diameter: 70px and Hardness: 50%. Also, ensure that the Opacity and Flow options are set at 100% in the options bar.

D. Hold down the Alt key, and click in an area on the hills in the background. That area has now been selected as the clone source.

E. Click several times within the selection to remove its contents. You can click and drag in small areas throughout the roof until it is completely filled with the background.

F. Press Ctrl+D (PC) or Command+D (Mac) to remove the selection.

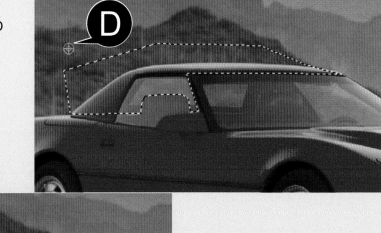

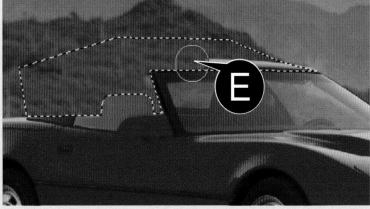

STEP 4 : ADJUSTING BRIGHTNESS

The area of the passenger seat that was previously behind glass is duller than the rest of
the image. To fix this, we'll select the area
and then adjust its brightness levels.

A. Click the Zoom Tool button.

B. Click and drag around the dull area of the
car.

C. Click and hold the Polygon Lasso Tool
button. A list of tools will appear.

D. Click the Lasso Tool option.

E. Click the "New selection" button.

F. Enter "0" in the Feather box in the options bar.

G. Click and drag around the dull area.
When you release your mouse button, a
marquee will appear around the selected
area.

H. Click Image | Adjustments |
Brightness/Contrast. The
Brightness/Contrast dialog box will now
appear.

I. Click and drag the sliders to enter the
following settings: Brightness: -75 and
Contrast: 0.

J. Click OK to close the dialog box and
apply the settings.

K. Press Ctrl+D (PC) or Command+D
(Mac) to remove the
selection.

L. Press Ctrl+0 (PC) or
Command+0 (Mac) to
zoom to full view.

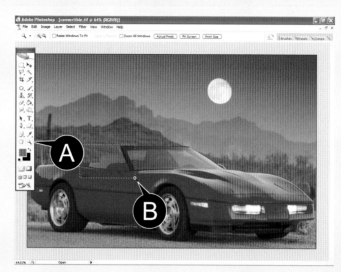

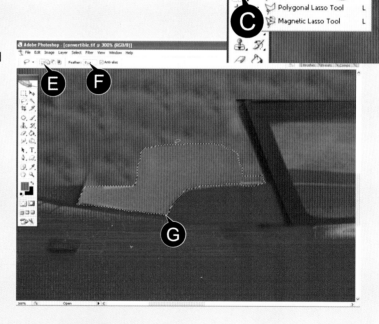

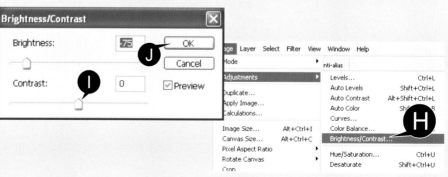

Reflection

14

Greek mythology tells us the story of Narcissus, a young man who falls in love with his own reflection. If you have a photograph of a sweet car like the one pictured above, you may want to create a reflection so that it too can fall in love with itself. The process of creating a reflection is really quite simple. The reflection itself is just a slightly modified copy of the original image. After you've selected and copied the image, you will flip it and then change its opacity to make the reflection look authentic. This technique is also great to use on images of landscapes and skylines.

Project Files

The file for this project is called reflection.tif and can be found at: www.mimosabooks.com/files

Completion Time

After the files have been downloaded, this project should take approximately five minutes to ten minutes to complete.

Degree of Difficulty

☆☆

Project Tools

Move Tool

Lasso Tool

Palettes

Ensure the following palettes, which can be accessed from the Window menu, are open for this project:

Tools

STEP 1 : OPEN THE TUTORIAL

Before we can get any work done, we need to first open the file we'll be using in this project.

A. Press Ctrl+O (PC) or Command+O (Mac) to launch the Open dialog box.

B. Browse to the folder where you saved the tutorial files.

C. Click on the file entitled "reflection.tif." It will be highlighted.

D. Click the Open button. The file will open.

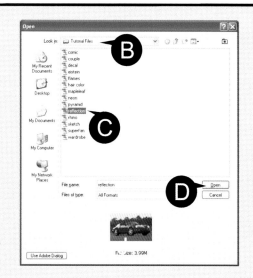

STEP 2 : ISOLATING THE CAR

The reflection itself is made of only the car, so it will need to be isolated. We'll be using the Lasso tool to select the car. The good news is that we don't need to be extremely accurate when creating the selection.

A. Click the Lasso Tool button. If the Lasso Tool button isn't present (for example, you may see the Magnetic Lasso Tool button in the same location), click and hold the button, and then select the Lasso Tool option.

B. Type "2" in the Feather box in the options bar.

C. Click and drag around the outside edge of the car. Don't worry about being too exact -- just get as close as you can. When you release the mouse button, a series of "marching ants" will appear around the car.

D. Press Ctrl+J (PC) or Command+J (Mac) twice. This will copy your selection onto two separate layers.

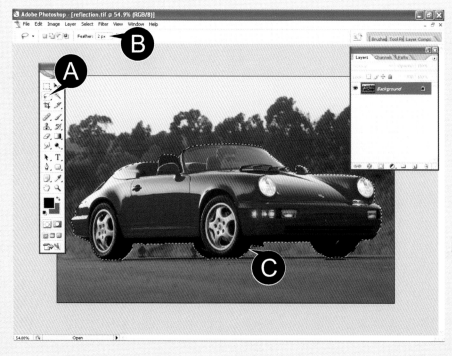

STEP 3 : SKEWING THE CAR

To make the reflection, we need to resize and skew one of the copies of the car. We'll do this using the Move tool.

A. Click on Layer 1. It will now be highlighted.

B. Click on the Move Tool button. A series of white handles will appear around the car.

C. Position your mouse pointer over the top middle handle. You'll know you're over the handle when your mouse pointer changes into a double-sided arrow.

D. Click and drag downward, past the bottom of the car, until your mouse pointer is at the bottom of the image.

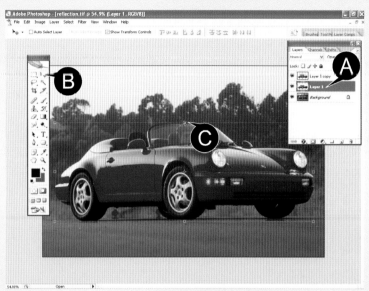

STEP 3 : SKEWING THE CAR CONT.

E. Position the mouse pointer over the middle of the reflection car. Click and drag it until the tires match up with one another. If you find that the movement isn't smooth, when you are dragging the reflection, the snap feature may be on. You can turn this off by clicking View | Snap.

F. Click Edit | Transform | Skew. You will now be able to skew the image.

G. Position your mouse pointer over the bottom-middle handle. Click and drag slightly to the left to skew the image.

H. Click the Commit button on the options bar.

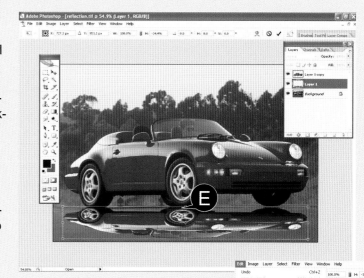

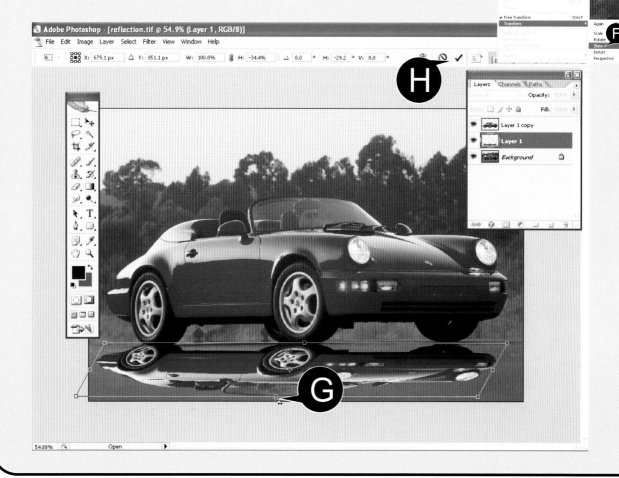

STEP 4 : APPLYING EFFECTS

To perfect our reflection, we are going to adjust its opacity level so that the road underneath shows through slightly. We are also going to apply a ripple effect to finish off the reflection.

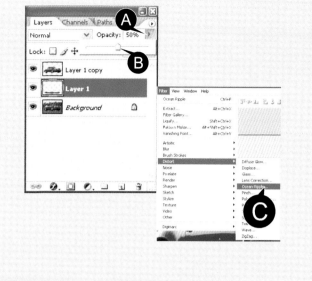

A. Click the Opacity drop-down arrow in the Layers palette. A slider bar will appear.

B. Click and drag the slider until the opacity level reaches 50%.

C. Click Filter | Distort | Ocean Ripple. You will now be able to enter settings for this effect. The dialog box you see may appear different than the one shown here, depending on which version of Photoshop you are using.

D. Click and drag the sliders to enter the following values: Ripple Size: 2, Ripple Magnitude: 2.

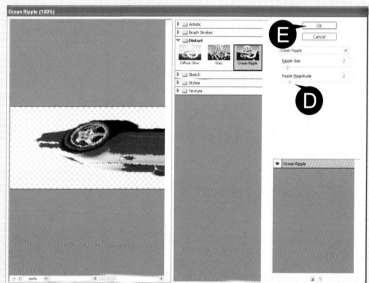

E. Click OK. The effect will be applied.

F. Click Image | Adjustments | Brightness/Contrast. The Brightness/Contrast dialog box will appear.

G. Click and drag the sliders to the following levels: Brightness: -50, Contrast: +50.

H. Click OK. The settings will be applied. Your reflection is now complete.

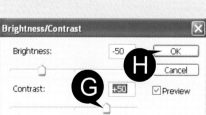

Need For
Speed

Project Files

The file for this project is called speed.tif and can be found at:
www.mimosabooks.com/files

Completion Time

After the files have been downloaded, this project should take approximately ten minutes to fifteen minutes to complete.

Degree of Difficulty

☆☆☆

Project Tools

✎ Eraser Tool

◯ Lasso Tool

Palettes

Ensure the following palettes, which can be accessed from the Window menu, are open for this project:

Tools

Layers

Scientific studies have shown that certain people who love risk-taking and danger have an imbalance of an enzyme called MAO. For the rest of us, who are afraid of great risks but still want to create the illusion of danger and speed, we can follow this project. Here we will create the illusion of motion by applying a blur filter. We are also going to create artificial smoke, billowing from the tires, and the look of acceleration. You can apply the techniques in this project to just about any photograph of a motionless car, boat, motorcycle, or person.

STEP 1 : OPEN THE TUTORIAL

Before we can get any work done, we need to first open the file we'll need for this project.

A. Press Ctrl+O (PC) or Command+O (Mac) to launch the Open dialog box.

B. Browse to the folder where you saved the tutorial files.

C. Click on the file entitled "speed.tif." It will be highlighted.

D. Click the Open button. The file will open.

E. Click the Maximize button to expand the window.

F. Press Ctrl+0 (PC) or Command+0 (Mac) to zoom to full view.

G. Press Ctrl+J (PC) or Command+J (Mac) to create a duplicate of the Background layer that you'll use as a working layer.

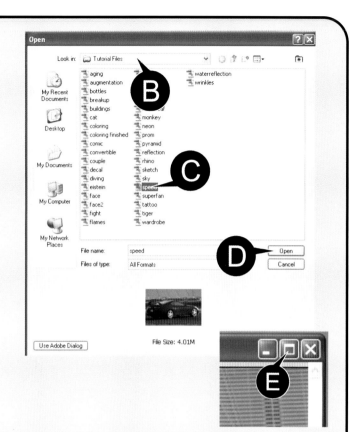

NOTES

STEP 2 : CREATING A MOTION BLUR

We are going to isolate specific areas of the image and create a blur in those areas using the Motion Blur filter.

A. Click the Lasso Tool button.

B. Click the "New selection" button if it is not already selected.

C. Type "3" in the Feather box.

D. Click and drag around the car but do not include the front or back tire. When you release the mouse button, a marquee will appear around the area you selected.

E. Click Select | Inverse. Everything except the area you selected in Step C will now be the active selection.

F. Click Filter | Blur | Motion Blur. The Motion Blur dialog box will appear.

G. Click and drag the Distance slider to 25 pixels.

H. Click OK. The effect will be applied.

I. Press Ctrl+D (PC) or Command+D (Mac) to remove the selection.

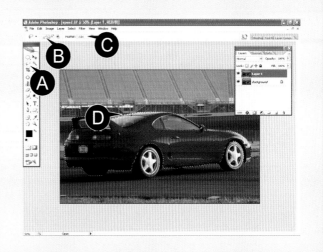

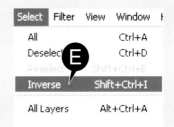

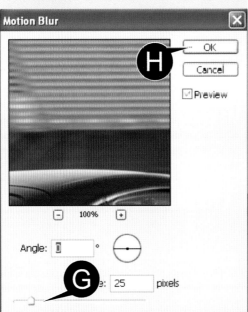

STEP 3 : ADDING SMOKE

We are going to create the illusion of smoke appearing from the tires as the car accelerates.

A. Click the "New layer" button in the Layers palette.

B. Press the letter "D" on the keyboard. This will revert the foreground and background color to their default status, black and white.

C. Click Filter | Render | Clouds. A black and white cloud-like image will appear.

D. Click the Eraser tool.

E. Click the Brush Preset picker arrow in the toolbar.

F. Click and drag the sliders to the following settings: Master Diameter: 250px, Hardness: 0%.

G. Click the Opacity arrow in the Layers palette to bring open the Opacity slider.

H. Click and drag the slider until it's 50%.

I. Click over all the areas of the clouds, except those areas behind the front and rear tires.

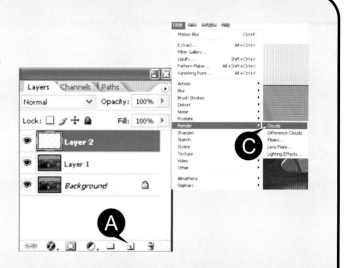

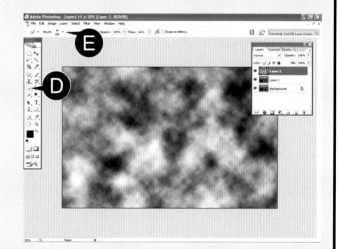

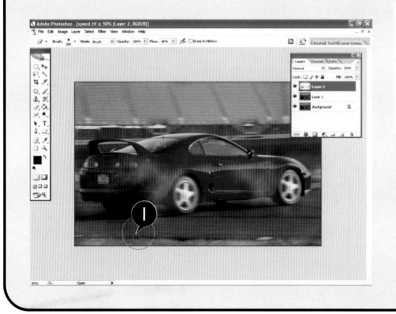

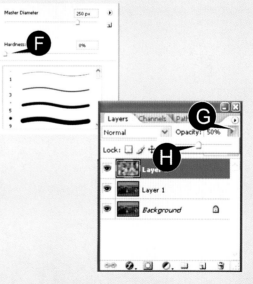

Hockey Fight

Growing up in Canada, whether we liked it or not, we were exposed in some way to hockey. Whether it was watching Hockey Night in Canada on Saturday nights, early morning hockey practices, or playing at the outdoor rink after school, hockey was part of life for most Canadian kids. Fortunately for me, my father kept me out of contact hockey so I could escape the bumps, bruises, and fights that some of my friends had to endure. Even though I avoided the fights, I can still create the illusion of the results of a hockey battle by using the various tools in Photoshop. I can guarantee that after completing this project, no Tylenol or bandages will be required.

Project Files

The file for this project is called fight.tif and can be found at:
www.mimosabooks.com/files

Completion Time

After the files have been downloaded, this project should take approximately ten minutes to fifteen minutes to complete.

Degree of Difficulty

Project Tools

Paint Bucket Tool
Smudge Tool
Zoom Tool
Eraser Tool
Lasso Tool
Burn Tool

Palettes

Ensure the following palettes, which can be accessed from the Window menu, are open for this project:

Tools
Layers
Colors

STEP 1 : OPEN THE TUTORIAL

Before we can get any work done, we need to first open the file we'll be using in this project.

A. Press Ctrl+O (PC) or Command+O (Mac) to launch the Open dialog box.

B. Browse to the folder where you saved the tutorial files.

C. Click on the file entitled "fight.tif." It will be high-lighted.

D. Click the Open button. The file will open.

E. Click the Maximize button to maximize the size of the window.

F. Press Ctrl+J (PC) or Command+J (Mac) to create a duplicate layer of the background layer to work on.

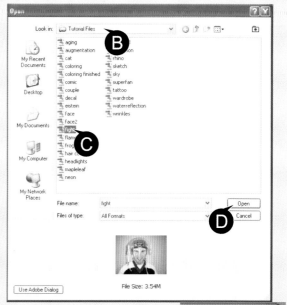

When moving an object, you may find that it doesn't move smoothly across the screen. If this is the case, the "Snap" feature may be turned on. To turn off this feature, click View and then deselect the Snap option.

STEP 2 : REMOVING A TOOTH

I can't imagine many things that would hurt more than being hit in the mouth with a hockey puck moving at 80 mph. It's a good thing that we don't have to endure that type of pain to create the look of someone that was hit by a puck. In this case, we'll simply select the area of the mouth we want to remove and then adjust the brightness and contrast settings. It'll be pain free -- guaranteed.

A. Click the Zoom Tool button.

B. Click and drag around the area of the mouth. As you drag, a marquee will appear, previewing the location of the new zoom region.

C. Click the Lasso Tool button.

D. Click the "New selection" button, if it isn't already selected.

E. Enter "2" in the Feather box in the options bar.

F. Click and drag around the man's front right tooth. When you release the mouse button, a series of "marching ants" will appear to display the selected region.

G. Click Image | Adjustments | Brightness/Contrast. The Brightness/Contrast dialog box will appear.

H. Click and drag the sliders until the settings are as follows: Brightness: -100, Contrast: +75.

I. Click OK. The settings will be applied to the tooth.

J. Press Ctrl+D (PC) or Command+D (Mac) to remove the selection.

K. Press Ctrl+0 (PC) or Command+0 (Mac) to zoom to full view.

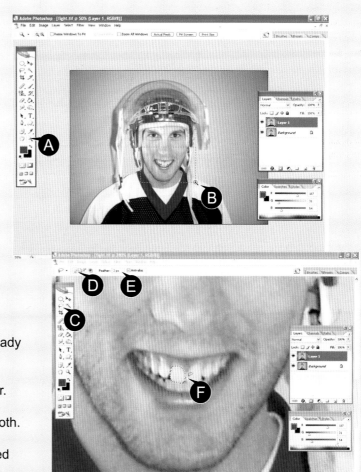

STEP 3 : MAKING A BLACK EYE

The after-effect of a good hockey fight is typically a black and blue eye. The Burn tool, which is typically used to touch up old photos, is great for creating a realistic "shiner."

A. Click and hold the Dodge Tool button. A series of tools will appear.

B. Click the Burn Tool option. Your options bar will change to offer options for the Burn tool.

C. Click the Brush Preset picker arrow. A menu with different options for the brush will appear.

D. Click and drag the sliders to set the following values: Master Diameter: 150px, Hardness: 0%.

E. Ensure the settings are as follows in the options bar: Range: Midtones and Exposure: 50%.

F. Click about 6-8 times over the man's left eye. Each time you click, the black eye will become slightly darker. It will also have a reddish outline.

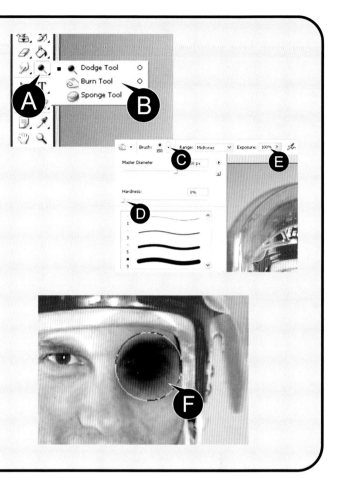

STEP 4 : TIDYING UP

Typically, a black eye doesn't include the eyeball, so we'll have to tidy up the effect we applied in the previous step. We'll do this using the Eraser tool.

A. Click the Eraser Tool button.

B. Click the Brush Preset picker arrow. A menu with different options for the brush will appear.

C. Click and drag the sliders to set the following values: Master Diameter: 20px, Hardness: 0%.

D. Ensure the settings are as follows in the options bar: Mode: Brush, Opacity: 50%, and Flow: 50%.

E. Click and drag over the man's eyeball. As you drag, the part of the black eye that is directly over the eyeball will be erased.

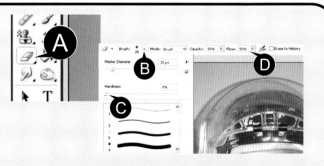

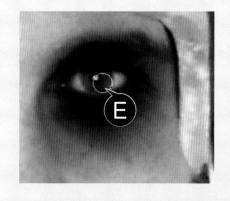

STEP 5 : CREATING THE SCAR

To create the scar, we'll make use of a variety of tools; but primarily it'll be the Smudge tool that we use to make the blood look realistic.

A. Click the Zoom Tool button.

B. Click and drag a marquee underneath the man's right eye.

C. Click the New Layer button in the Layers palette.

D. Click the Lasso Tool button.

E. Enter "0" in the Feather box in the options bar.

F. Click and drag a long, thin, oval shape selection under the man's eye.

G. Click on a reddish color in the Color palette.

H. Click the Paint Bucket Tool button.

I. Click anywhere within the selection; it will fill with the color you selected in Step G.

J. Press Ctrl+D (PC) or Command+D (Mac) to remove the selection.

K. Click the Smudge Tool button.

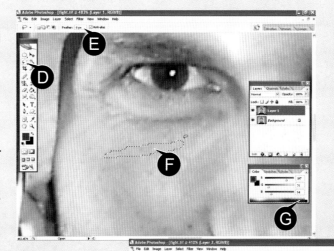

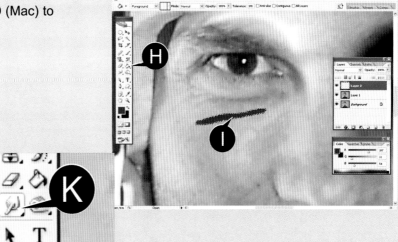

STEP 5 : CREATING THE BLOODY SCAR CONT.

L. Click the Brush Preset picker arrow. A menu with different options for the brush will appear.

M. Click and drag the sliders to set the following values: Master Diameter: 3px, Hardness: 0%.

N. Ensure the following settings are in the options bar: Mode: Normal and Strength: 75%.

O. Starting from the middle of the red area, click and drag downward slightly to smudge the scar. Here we are trying to create the illusion of the blood dripping slightly.

P. Repeat Step O for other areas along the scar.

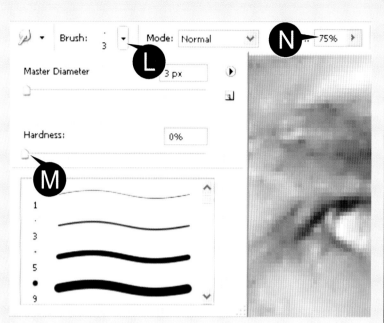

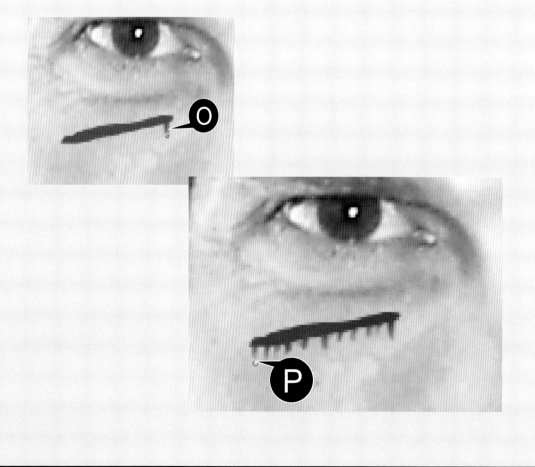

STEP 6 : FINISHING THE SCAR

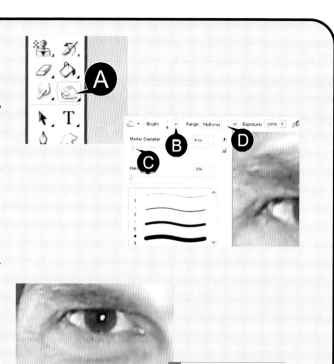

To give the scar some illusion of depth, we will make it darker in the middle using the Burn tool. After that, we'll apply a texture to it to make it look more real. Finally, we'll change the opacity level to make the scar blend into the skin.

A. Click the Burn Tool button.

B. Click the Brush Preset picker arrow. A menu with different options for the brush will appear.

C. Click and drag the sliders to set the following values: Master Diameter: 4px, Hardness: 0%.

D. Ensure the following settings are in the options bar: Range: Midtones and Exposure: 100%.

E. Click and drag across the middle of the scar. The area over which you drag will now be darker.

F. Click Filter | Texture | Texturizer. Depending on the version of Photoshop that you are using, either the Filter Gallery or the Texturizer dialog box will appear.

G. Click OK to accept the default settings.

H. Click the Opacity arrow in the Layers palette to bring up a slider that will allow you to adjust the opacity level of this layer.

I. Drag the slider until it reaches 70%.

J. Press Ctrl+0 (PC) or Command+0 (Mac) to zoom out to full view. Your picture is now complete.

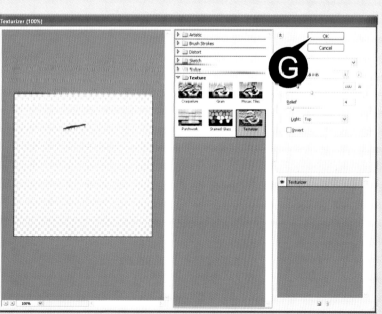

You Too Can Be Famous

17

My wife loves everything to do with celebrities. She loves watching them on entertainment TV shows, she loves reading about them in magazines, and above all she loves having her picture taken with them. I, on the other hand, couldn't be bothered with chasing after those that appear on TV. With this project, we both win, because I can put myself into a photo of any celebrity without having to chase them down or bother them. In this project, you'll not only learn the techniques used to extend a photograph to make room for yourself, you'll learn some techniques for making the doctored photograph look realistic.

Project Files

The files for this project are called einstein.tif and couple.tif and can be found at: www.mimosabooks.com/files

Completion Time

After the files have been downloaded, this project should take approximately fifteen minutes to twenty minutes to complete.

Degree of Difficulty

☆☆☆☆☆

Project Tools

⬚ Rectangular Marquee Tool

🪄 Magnetic Lasso Tool

🔗 Lasso Tool

➕ Move Tool

Palettes

Ensure the following palettes, which can be accessed from the Window menu, are open for this project:

Tools
Navigator
Layers

STEP 1 : OPEN THE TUTORIAL

Before we can get any work done, we need to first open the files we'll be using in this project.

A. Press Ctrl+O (PC) or Command+O (Mac) to launch the Open dialog box.

B. Browse to the folder where you saved the tutorial files.

C. Click on the file entitled "einstein.tif." It will be highlighted.

D. Hold down the Ctrl key and click on the file marked "couple.tif." It too will now be highlighted.

E. Click the Open button. The files will open, and the file einstein.tif will be the active image, because it was selected first when opening the images.

F. Click the Maximize button to have the window fill the entire screen.

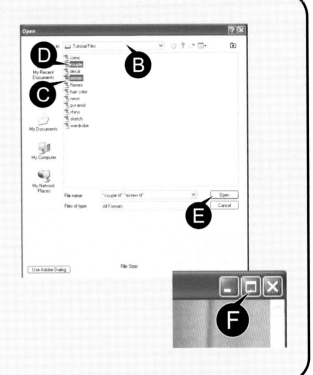

STEP 2 : EXPANDING THE CANVAS

In order to make room for the person we are going to be adding to the image, we need to expand the canvas. When expanding a canvas in Photoshop, you select exactly where and by how much you'd like the canvas increased. In this case we will be adding some additional space to the left of Einstein.

A. Click Image | Canvas Size. The Canvas Size dialog box will open.

B. Click on the drop-down arrow and select "inches" if it doesn't already appear as the unit of measurement.

C. Type the number "11" for the width of the new canvas.

D. Click on the middle arrow on the right to indicate that you would like the additional space added to the left of the document.

E. Click OK. You will now see that additional space has been added to the left of the image.

F. Press Ctrl+J (PC) or Command+J (Mac) to make a copy of the image on a separate layer. It's always a good idea to do your image editing on a separate layer.

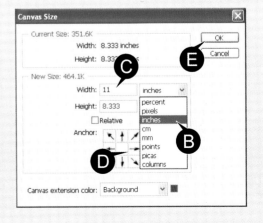

STEP 3 : FILLING THE BACKGROUND

In order to be consistent we want the background of the new area of the canvas that we added in the previous step to be the same as the background in the original picture. Photoshop provides us with a variety of options for cloning an area, but perhaps the easiest is simply to cut and paste.

A. Click and hold the Marquee Tool button. A list of different options will appear.

B. Click the Rectangular Marquee Tool button.

C. Click and drag the Zoom slider in the Navigator palette until it reaches about 74%.

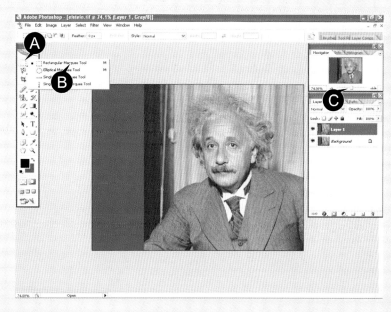

D. Click and drag over an area to the right of Einstein's head. Make sure that your selection begins from the top of the image and includes only background. If you make a mistake while creating the selection you can click Ctrl+Z (PC) or Command+Z (Mac) to undo your last step and then you can start the selection again.

E. Press Ctrl+C (PC) or Command+C (Mac) to copy the selection.

F. Press Ctrl+V (PC) or Command+V (Mac) to paste the selection. It will be pasted on a new layer.

G. Click the Move Tool button. A series of handles will appear around your object.

H. Click and drag the object so that it is over the darker area of the background.

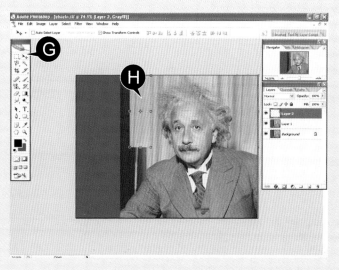

STEP 3 : FILLING CONT.

I. Position your mouse pointer over the bottom middle handle and drag down until the shape is stretched
and is partially covering Einstein's shoulder. We are
not stretching it all the way to the bottom because we
don't want the object to appear too distorted. Plus,
the image we will be pasting later will cover the bottom area anyways.

J. Click the Commit button in the options bar.

K. Click View | Snap. This will turn off the Snap fea-
ture if it is turned on and allow you to freely move
your objects. The check mark beside the word
"Snap" in the menu indicates that this feature is on.

L. Press Ctrl+J (PC) or Command+J (Mac) to make
an exact copy of this layer.

M. Click the Move Tool button. A series of handles
will appear around your object.

N. Click and drag the object to the left so that it
slightly overlaps the original object.

O. Repeat Steps L - N two more times so that entire
extra background that
you created earlier is
covered.

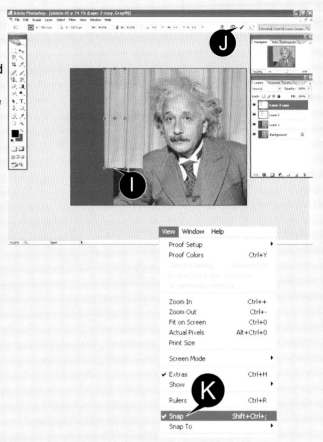

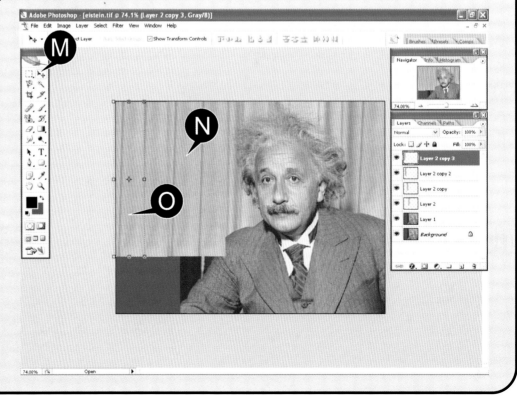

STEP 4 : MERGING LAYERS

In the previous step, when you pasted the object to create a background, each object was created on its own separate layer. Rather than having to manage so many different layers, we can merge them into one.

A. Hold down the Shift key and click on Layer 1. All of the layers, except for the Background layer, will be selected.

B. Click Layer | Merge Layers. All of the layers that are selected will be merged together.

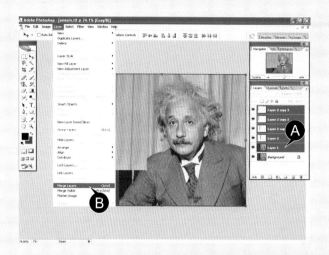

STEP 5 : ISOLATING THE MAN

The man that we are going to place together with Einstein needs to be removed from the picture that he is currently in. To do this, we will create a selection that isolates only him, using the Magnetic Lasso tool.

A. Click Window | couple.tif. The couple image will become active.

B. Click and hold the Lasso Tool button to see a list of different selection tools.

C. Click the Magnetic Lasso Tool option.

D. Type the number "1" in the Feather box.

E. Click and drag around the outside edge of the man. As you drag, a line with little nodes around it should cling to the edge of the man. You can also click as you drag to anchor some points on the line.

F. Double-click when you reach the point where you started. A selection, represented by a series of "marching ants," will appear around the man.

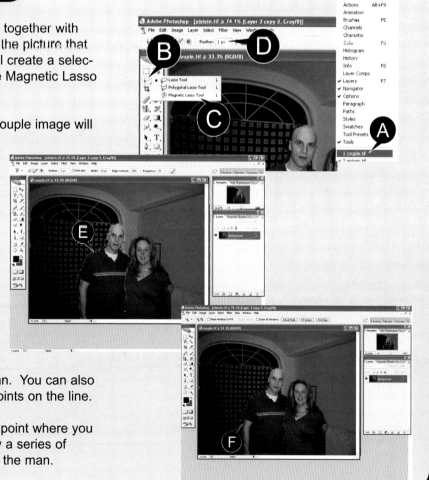

STEP 6 : ADJUSTING

While the Magnetic Lasso tool did a great job of isolating the image, it isn't perfect. We'll use the Lasso tool to add to and subtract from different parts of our selection that need to be adjusted.

A. Click the Zoom Tool button.

B. Click and drag around an area that needs to be included in the selection, but was missed when you first created the selection. As you drag, a marquee will appear. You will now be zoomed in closely around that area.

C. Click and hold the Lasso tool button to see a list of different selection tools.

D. Click the Lasso Tool option.

E. Click the "Add to selection" button in the options bar. This will put you into additive mode, so any area you drag around will be added to your selection.

F. Click and drag around an area that you would like to add to the selection. When you release your mouse button, the area you dragged around will be added to the selection.

G. Press Ctrl+0 (PC) or Command+0 (Mac) to zoom out to full view again.

H. Repeat Steps A - G for any other areas you would like to add to your selection.

I. Click the "Subtract from selection" button in the options bar. This will put you into subtractive mode so that any area you drag around will be removed from your selection.

J. Click and drag around an area that you would like to remove from the selection. When you release your mouse button, the area you dragged around will be removed from the selection. You may have to zoom in to get a better view. Steps A - B above cover how to zoom into a specific area.

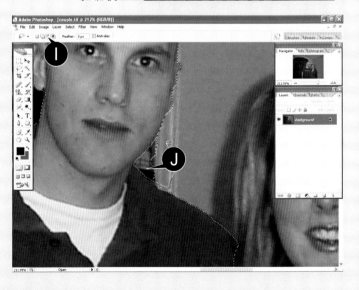

STEP 6 : ADJUSTING CONT.

K. Press Ctrl+0 (PC) or Command+0 (Mac) to zoom out to full view again.

L. Repeat Steps I - J for any other areas you would like to remove from your selection.

M. Press Ctrl+C (PC) or Command+C (Mac) to copy the selection to the clipboard.

N. Click Window | einstein.tif to switch to the Einstein image.

STEP 7 : INSERTING THE IMAGE

Now that the image is on the clipboard, we need to paste it on our image of Einstein. We'll then resize it to fit in proportion to the image.

A. Press Ctrl+V (PC) or Command+V (Mac) to paste the image. It will appear on a separate layer.

B. Click on the Move Tool button. A series of handles will appear around the pasted object.

C. Click and drag the image of the man until it is to the left of Einstein.

D. Position your mouse pointer over one of the corner handles and drag inward slightly to reduce the size of the image of the man.

E. Click and drag the image to reposition the man so that he slightly overlaps Einstein's arm.

F. Click the Commit button on the options bar.

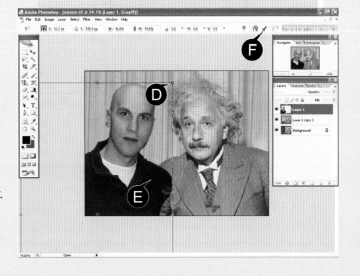

STEP 8 : ADJUSTING LEVELS

Although the image is in black and white, the image of the man appears slightly darker than that of Einstein. This can be quickly corrected by adjusting the levels.

A. Click Image | Adjustments | Auto Levels. The levels in the image will be adjusted, and it will appear lighter.

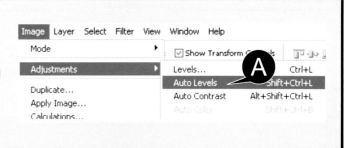

PHOTOGRAPHY 101

The Perfect Family Portrait - There are a few key elements that, if followed, will make a huge difference in the appearance of your portraits. One of the keys to a great portrait is to be aware of the background. Simpler backgrounds are better, because you don't want objects in the background distracting from the main image. Rather than having people line up in a straight line, organize them in a particular shape, such as a circle or triangle. Also, make sure that everyone in the picture is connected in some way, either by slightly touching or being attached to an object, such as a rock or chair. Follow these instructions and you're one step closer to the perfect family portrait.

When using the Lasso tool to create selections, you can either draw freehand by clicking and dragging or set anchor points by clicking once at the points where you'd like the anchors to appear. Pressing the Delete key as you create a selection will remove the last part of the line segment that was drawn.

STEP 9 : CHANGING ORDER

Currently it appears as though Einstein is behind the
man that we pasted. Considering that
the man's arm is cut off anyway, in this
step, we will make it appear as though
Einstein is in front of the man.

A. Click the eye-shaped icon beside the
layer where the man was pasted. This
layer will now be invisible.

B. Click the eye-shaped icon beside the
layer where the background was extended. This layer will now be invisible.

C. Click on the Background layer in the
Layers palette. It will be highlighted.

D. Click the Lasso Tool button.

E. Click and drag around Einstein's arm
and part of his jacket.

F. Press Ctrl+C (PC) or Command+C (Mac). The
selection will be copied.

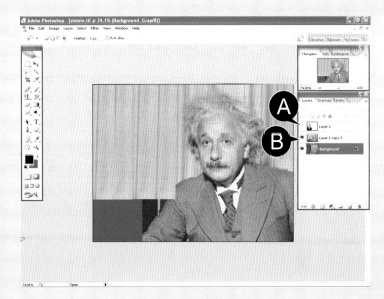

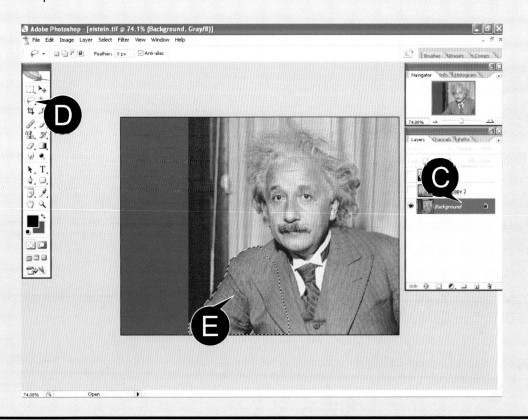

STEP 9 : CHANGING ORDER CONT.

G. Press Ctrl+D (PC) or Command+D (Mac) to remove the selection.

H. Click on the eye-shaped icon beside the image of the man and Layer 2. Those layers will become visible.

I. Click on the layer with the pasted man. It will be highlighted.

J. Press Ctrl+V (PC) or Command+V (Mac) to paste the arm.

K. Click the Move Tool button. The arm you pasted will have a series of handles surrounding it.

L. Click and drag the arm to align it with Einstein's body. That's it, you're done!

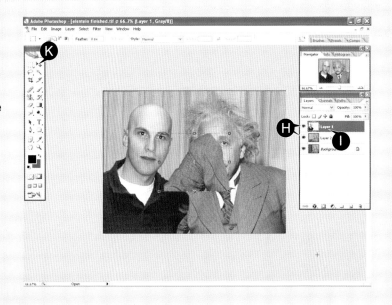

Breaking Up
Is Easy To Do

Project Files

The file for this project is called breakup.tif and can be found at: www.mimosabooks.com/files

Completion Time

After the files have been downloaded, this project should take approximately ten minutes to twenty minutes to complete.

Degree of Difficulty

☆☆☆☆☆

Project Tools

Patch Tool

Crop Tool

Clone Stamp Tool

Palettes

Ensure the following palettes, which can be accessed from the Window menu, are open for this project:

Tools

There's really nothing much worse than the process of going through a breakup with someone. The pictures of you and your mate around the house are constant reminders of how something so right went so wrong. The problem with throwing out those photos is that you just look so darn good in some of those shots, and it would be a crying shame to waste them. Not to worry -- Photoshop to the rescue! In Photoshop, you can remove unwanted elements, including people, with relative ease. There are a variety of tools that you can use to remove an object and then replace it with other elements of the background. This project primarily uses the Patch and Clone Stamp tools to replicate the background and remove the unwanted man.

STEP 1 : OPEN THE TUTORIAL

Before we can get any work done, we need to first open the file we'll be using in this project.

A. Press Ctrl+O (PC) or Command+O (Mac) to launch the Open dialog box.

B. Browse to the folder where you saved the tutorial files.

C. Click on the file entitled "breakup.tif." It will be highlighted.

D. Click the Open button. The file will open.

E. Click the Maximize button to expand the window to its full size.

F. Press Ctrl+J (PC) or Command+J (Mac) to create a working layer.

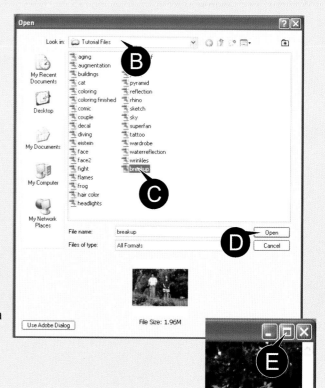

PHOTOGRAPHY 101

Outdoor Flash - Most people think that they should only use the flashes on their cameras when taking pictures indoors or at night. The truth of the matter is that using your flash can be very effective when taking pictures outdoors in bright sunlight. The problem with some pictures taken in bright sunlight is that the sun can cast some very dark shadows, which could make portions of your photograph difficult to see. By using the flash on these outdoor photos, the shadows will be eliminated. Ultimately, the flash will add contrast to your photo and will improve its overall quality.

Since most people use their flashes in automatic mode, you will probably have to manually set the flash to fire when taking an outdoor picture. Consult the manual that came with your camera to determine how to adjust the flash settings.

STEP 2 : REMOVING THE MAN

To remove the man, we'll make use of the Patch tool. While the Patch tool is ideal for small areas, we can still use it to remove the large area of the man and later clean up the details.

A. Click and hold the button under the Crop Tool button. A list of different options will appear.

B. Click the Patch Tool option.

C. Ensure that the Source option is selected in the options bar.

D. Click and drag around the man. When you release the mouse button, a selection marquee will appear.

E. Position the mouse pointer over the selection. The mouse pointer will have a small rectangle attached to it.

F. Click and drag the selection to the clear area on the far right of the screen. As you drag, a preview of the area over which your cursor is hovering will appear in the selection. Try to align the horizontal lines of the ground. When you release the mouse button, the man will disappear. It won't yet be perfect, but we'll clean it up in the next step.

G. Press Ctrl+D (PC) or Command+D (Mac) to remove the selection.

STEP 3 : TIDYING UP THE MAN

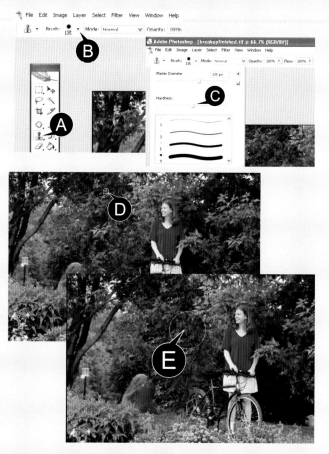

While the man has been removed, it still looks like the ghost of the man exists and is haunting the picture. We'll use the Clone Stamp tool to replicate some of the background over the "ghost" to clean it up.

A. Click the Clone Stamp Tool button.

B. Click the Brush Preset picker arrow on the options bar.

C. Click and drag the sliders to enter the following settings: Master Diameter: 135px, Hardness: 50%. Also, be sure that the Opacity and Flow options are set at 100% in the options bar.

D. Hold down the Alt key and click on a blank green area above the "ghost."

E. Click several times around the ghost to clone the area you selected in Step D.

F. Repeat Steps D-E with several other areas to create a random look to the background. Also click over the blurred area of the rock.

STEP 4 : CROPPING THE IMAGE

Now that the man has been removed, the woman seems off center. To correct this, we'll crop part of the image.

A. Click the Crop Tool button.

B. Click and drag around the part of the image that you would like to keep. Don't worry if you don't get it perfect, as it will be adjusted in the next step. When you release the mouse button, a dark area will surround the area that will be removed from the image.

C. Click and drag over any of the white box handles to adjust the crop area.

D. Press the Enter or Return key to crop the image. Alternatively, you can click the Commit button on the options bar.

Be Your Own
Comic Book
Hero

Project Files

The file for this project is called comic.tif and can be found at:
www.mimosabooks.com/files

Completion Time

After the files have been downloaded, this project should take approximately five minutes to ten minutes to complete.

Degree of Difficulty

☆☆

Project Tools

This project uses only filters so there are no tools required.

Palettes

No windows or palettes are needed for this project.

Do you have a favorite comic book hero? Is it Spiderman? Batman? Wonder Woman? The real heroes in life are all around us -- our friends, coworkers, family, and neighbors. Using Photoshop, you can make anyone into a comic book hero simply by applying a few filters. Filters act as special effects that you can apply to a photograph that will allow you, amongst other things, to convert any person into a comic book character. If you are using versions CS or CS2, you can use the Filter Gallery, which allows you to apply multiple filters without having to access different dialog boxes. If you are using version 7 you will have to apply these filters one at a time.

STEP 1 : OPEN THE TUTORIAL

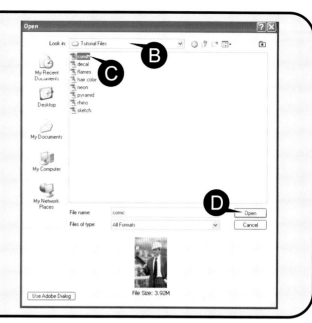

Before we can get any work done, we need to first open the file we'll need for this project.

A. Press Ctrl+O (PC) or Command+O (Mac) to launch the Open dialog box.

B. Browse to the folder where you saved the tutorial files.

C. Click on the file entitled "comic.tif." It will be highlighted.

D. Click the Open button. The file will open.

STEP 2 : PREPARING THE IMAGE

It's always a good idea to maximize an image, especially if you are working with one file. This will provide you with a better view of your image.

A. Click the Maximize button. The window containing the image will expand to the full size of the user interface.

When applying certain modifications, like moving or resizing an object, you can always press the "Cancel transformation" button on the options bar to cancel any modifications that you have applied. The "Cancel transformation" button looks like a "no smoking" sign without the cigarette.

STEP 3 : APPLYING FILTERS

The Filter Gallery is a window that allows you to apply multiple filters (also known as effects) to an image, all at once. Rather than having to individually apply filters, you can apply many at one time with this handy tool. The Filter Gallery was first introduced in version CS, so if you're using version 7, you'll have to apply the following filters manually.

A. Click Flter | Filter Gallery. The Filter Gallery will open.

B. Click on any filters listed after the very first one. Photoshop remembers the last filters that were applied with the Filter Gallery, so, if there is more than one listed, you'll have to select the extras and then delete them in order to start new.

C. Click the "Delete effect layer" button. The selected effect will be removed.

D. Repeat Steps B - C if there are any extra effects listed. When there is only one in the window, you are ready to proceed.

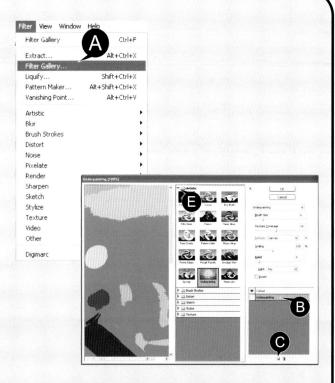

E. Click the arrow beside Artistic to expand the Artistic filters, if they are not already expanded. A triangle pointing down beside the folder name indicates that the folder has been expanded.

F. Click Poster Edges. The Poster Edges effect will be applied to your image, and you'll be able to adjust the settings for this effect.

G. Enter the following settings in the respective boxes, or click and drag the appropriate slider to enter: Edge Thickness: 1, Edge Intensity: 1, and Posterization: 1.

H. Click on the "New effect layer" button. This will allow you to apply a new effect to the same images.

I. Click Cutout. This effect will now be applied, and you'll be able to adjust its settings.

J. Enter the following settings in the respective boxes, or click and drag the appropriate slider to enter: Number of Levels: 3, Edge Simplicity: 3, and Edge Fidelity: 3.

K. Click OK. You'll be returned to your image.

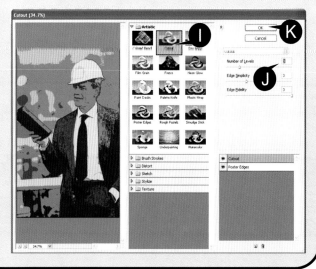

STEP 4 : APPLYING OTHER FIL-

Unfortunately, not every filter can be applied with the Filter Gallery. Some effects need to be applied manually. In this case, we will add one more effect to perfect our image.

A. Click Filter | Noise | Add Noise. The Add Noise dialog box will appear.

B. Enter "13" for the amount.

C. Click the radio button beside Uniform, if it's not already selected.

D. Uncheck the Monochromatic box, if it is selected.

E. Click OK. The effect will be applied.

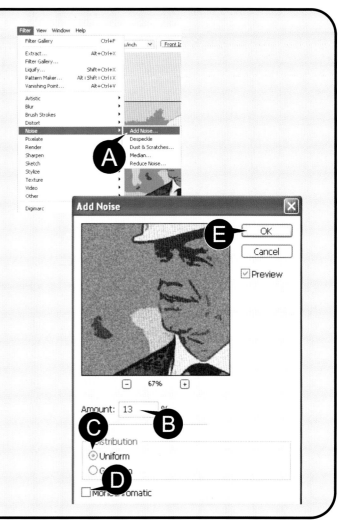

NOTES

Create Your Own
Old-Fashioned
Photos

Project Files

The file for this project is called old.tif and can be found at:
www.mimosabooks.com/files

Completion Time

After the files have been downloaded, this project should take approximately ten minutes to fifteen minutes to complete.

Degree of Difficulty

☆☆☆

Project Tools

- 🔲 Gradient Tool
- 🖊 Magic Wand Tool
- 🔍 Zoom Tool
- 〰 Lasso Tool
- ✋ Burn Tool

Palettes

Ensure the following palettes, which can be accessed from the Window menu, are open for this project:

Tools

Layers

I'm sure that somewhere in your house you've got a box of old photographs that have begun to show the signs of aging. So much attention is given to fixing and converting old photographs to make them look new. But what if you want to go the other way around? Through the use of a variety of effects and features, Photoshop gives you all the tools you need to make a new photograph look old. Why wait decades for a photo to become tattered-looking and aged, when you can accomplish the same effect in seconds?

STEP 1 : OPEN THE TUTORIAL

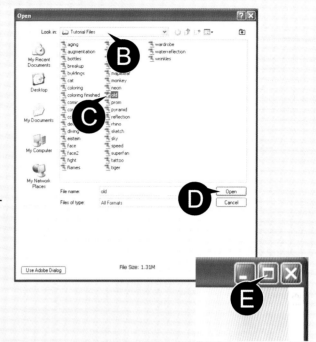

Before we can get any work done, we need to first open the file we'll be using in this project.

A. Press Ctrl+O (PC) or Command+O (Mac) to launch the Open dialog box.

B. Browse to the folder where you saved the tutorial files.

C. Click on the file entitled "old.tif." It will be highlighted.

D. Click the Open button. The file will open.

E. Click the Maximize button to maximize the size of the window.

F. Press Ctrl+0 (PC) or Command+0 (Mac) to zoom to the entire length and width of the picture.

NOTES

STEP 2 : CHANGING THE LIGHTING

Older cameras weren't nearly as sophisticated as the ones we currently have that can create bright, evenly-lit photographs. To change the lighting in this photo and to make it seem as though it was taken with an older camera, we'll apply a gradient fill to a new layer and then change the blending mode.

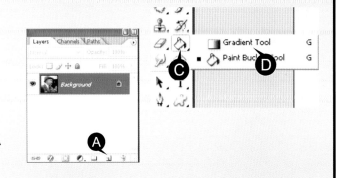

A. Click the New layer button in the Layers palette. A new blank layer will be created.

B. Press the letter "D" on the keyboard to revert to the default fill colors.

C. Click and hold the Paint Bucket Tool button to see a list of different fill tools.

D. Click the Gradient Tool option.

E. Click the Radial Gradient button in the options bar.

F. Ensure that all the check boxes, including Reverse, are checked in the options bar.

G. Click and drag outward starting at the center of the man's face to any of the corners. When you release the mouse button, you will be left with a radial fill that is white in the middle and dark around the edges.

H. Click the blending modes arrow in the Layers palette.

I. Click Multiply. The layers will be blended together.

J. Press Ctrl+E (PC) or Command+E (Mac) to combine the layers together.

STEP 3 : CHANGING THE COLORS

Another characteristic of some older photographs is that, rather than being in full color, they started off in black and white and then got discolored over the years. We'll recreate this effect by applying a duotone to our image.

A. Click Image | Mode | Grayscale. This will remove the color from your image and convert it to grayscale.

B. Click OK, if a dialog box appears confirming that you would like to remove the colors from the image.

C. Click Image | Mode | Duotone. The duotone dialog box will appear.

D. Click the arrow to expand the menu of options and select Duotone.

E. Click on the second fill box. Another dialog box will open from which you can select a color.

F. Click on a yellow hue in the bar.

G. Click OK. The color will be applied to the fill box.

H. Click OK. Your image will now have a duotone effect.

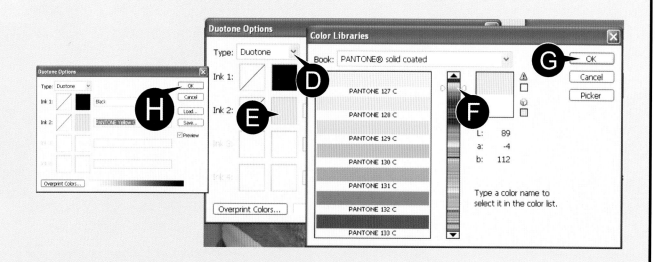

STEP 4 ; ADDING NOISE

Older photographs certainly weren't as crystal clear as the professional photo we are working with. To create a rougher look, we'll add some noise to a separate layer and then apply it to our image.

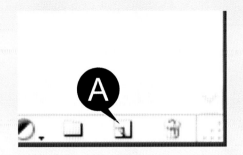

A. Click the New Layer button in the Layers palette. A new, separate layer will be created.

B. Click Edit | Fill. The Fill dialog box will appear.

C. Click the Use drop-down arrow and select White.

D. Click OK. The layer will now be filled with white.

E. Click Filter | Noise | Add Noise. This will open the Noise dialog box.

F. Click the Gaussian option.

G. Click and drag the Amount slider all the way to the right until 400% is in the Amount box.

H. Click OK. Noise will be applied to the layer.

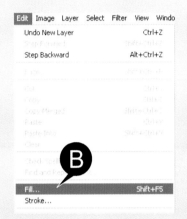

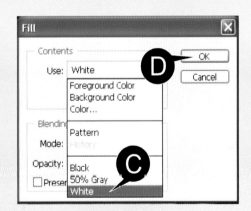

STEP 4 : ADDING NOISE CONT.

I. Click the Zoom Tool button.

J. Click and drag around a small area of the image to zoom in tightly.

K. Click the Magic Wand Tool button.

L. Ensure that the Contiguous option is not checked in the options bar and that the Tolerance level is 20.

M. Click on any white pixel. All the white pixels in the image will be selected.

N. Press the Delete key on your keyboard to remove all of the white pixels.

O. Press Ctrl+0 (PC) or Command+0 (Mac) to zoom out of the image.

P. Press Ctrl+D (PC) or Command+D to remove the selection.

Q. Click the Opacity arrow in the Layers palette. A slider will appear.

R. Click and drag it until the opacity level is 15%.

S. Press Ctrl+E (PC) or Command+E (Mac) to combine this layer with the background.

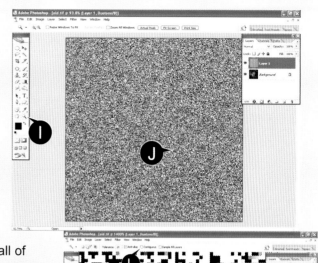

STEP 5 : ADDING A BORDER

We are going to roughen the border and slightly burn the edges to make the photo look more weathered.

A. Click the Lasso Tool button.

B. Click the New selection button in the options bar if it is not already selected.

C. Enter "1" in the Feather box.

D. Click and drag near the edge around the entire image. When you release the mouse button, a selection marquee will appear.

E. Click Select | Inverse. The selection will be inverted and only a small-framed selection will appear around the image.

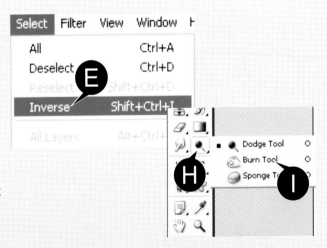

F. Press the Delete key to remove the contents of the selection from the image.

G. Press Ctrl+D (PC) or Command+D (Mac) to remove the selection.

H. Click and hold the Dodge Tool button to see a list of different tools.

I. Click the Burn Tool option.

J. Click the Brush Preset picker button.

K. Click and drag the sliders to the following settings: Master Diameter: 40px and Hardness: 0%. Also ensure that the Exposure box is at 100%.

L. Click and drag over a few areas around the edges to slightly burn the them. That's it, you're all done.

Gnome In A Bottle

If you take a second look at the image on the right above, you'll notice that inside the clear bottle is a garden gnome. The trick to this project is making the gnome appear as if it is actually inside the bottle. After isolating and copying the gnome from a different image, you'll paste and resize him into the image of the bottles. Then, by copying and pasting certain elements of the bottle, you'll create the illusion that he is actually within the bottle. To finalize the look, you'll adjust the layer opacity to really make the gnome look like he is behind glass.

Project Files

The files for this project are called bottles.tif and gnome.tif and can be found at:
www.mimosabooks.com/files

Completion Time

After the files have been downloaded, this project should take approximately five minutes to ten minutes to complete.

Degree of Difficulty

Project Tools

🔍 Zoom Tool

Magnetic Lasso Tool

Lasso Tool

Move Tool

Palettes

Ensure the following palettes, which can be accessed from the Window menu, are open for this project:

Tools
Navigator
Layers

STEP 1 : OPEN THE TUTORIAL

Before we can get any work done, we need to first open the files we'll need for this project. You can open multiple files at the same time within Photoshop. The order in which you select the files will determine the order in which they open. The file that you select first will be the active file when the files open.

A. Press Ctrl+O (PC) or Command+O (Mac) to launch the Open dialog box.

B. Browse to the folder where you saved the tutorial files.

C. Click on the file entitled "gnome.tif." It will be high-lighted.

D. Hold down the Ctrl key (PC) or Command key (Mac) and click on the file called "bottles.tif." It too will now be selected.

E. Click the Open button. Both files will open, but the gnome file will be active because it was the first file selected.

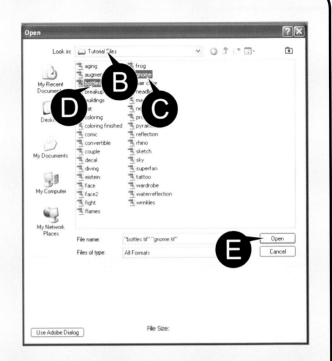

NOTES

STEP 2 : ISOLATING THE GNOME

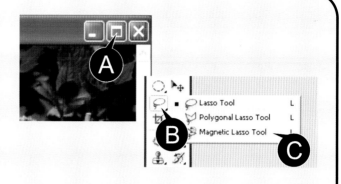

Our goal is to isolate the gnome so that we can bring it into our bottles picture. To do this, we are going to make use of the Magnetic Lasso tool.

A. Click the Maximize button to expand the window. This will make it easier to isolate the gnome.

B. Click and hold the Lasso Tool button. A list of different selection tools will appear.

C. Click the Magnetic Lasso Tool option.

D. Click and drag the Zoom slider in the Navigator palette until the gnome takes up most of the screen. A zoom level of approximately 86% should accomplish this.

E. Enter "1" in the Feather box.

F. Click and drag around the outside edge of the gnome. As you drag, a line with little nodes on it will appear, previewing the location of your selection. You can also click in certain points around the outside of the gnome to anchor the nodes. Don't worry if the line doesn't perfectly surround the gnome, we'll make little adjustments later in the process to perfect it.

G. Double-click once your line reaches the point where you started. A selection marquee will now appear around the gnome.

STEP 3 : TIDYING UP

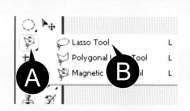

The Magnetic Lasso tool did a great job of creating a selection around the object, but it wasn't perfect. We can now add or take away from the selection using the Lasso tool.

A. Click and hold the Magnetic Lasso Tool button. A list of different selection tools will appear.

B. Click the Lasso Tool option.

C. Click the "Add to selection" button in the options bar. This will allow you to add areas to your selection.

D. Click and drag around any areas of the gnome that were not selected in your first selection attempt. When you release the mouse button, these areas will be selected.

E. Continue adding areas to the selection by clicking and dragging around them as required.

F. Click the "Subtract from selection" button on the options bar. This will allow you to remove areas from your selection.

G. Click and drag around any areas of the gnome that are part of your selection that you would like to remove. When you release the mouse button, these areas will be removed from the selection.

H. Repeat Steps C through G until the gnome is completely selected.

STEP 4 : TRANSPORTING

To bring the gnome into the bottle image, we will simply copy and paste it.

A. Press Ctrl+C (PC) or Command+C (Mac) to copy the selected gnome to the system clipboard.

B. Click Window | bottles.tif. This will switch the active window to the bottle image.

C. Click the Maximize button so that the bottle image takes up the entire window.

D. Press the Ctrl+V (PC) or Command+V (Mac) to paste the gnome into the image.

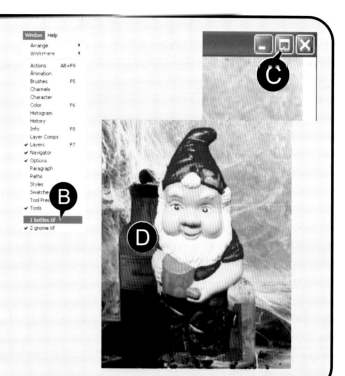

STEP 5 : POSITIONING THE GNOME

We are now going to reposition the gnome into the ideal location.

A. Click on the Move Tool button. A series of handles will appear around the gnome.

B. Position the mouse pointer over a corner node. Click and drag inward to resize the gnome until it is slightly smaller than the bottle.

C. Position the mouse pointer over the middle of the gnome. Click and drag it until it's right over the bottle.

D. Click the Commit button on the options bar.

E. Click the Zoom Tool button.

F. Click and drag a marquee around the smaller bottle. When you release the mouse button, you will be zoomed into that area.

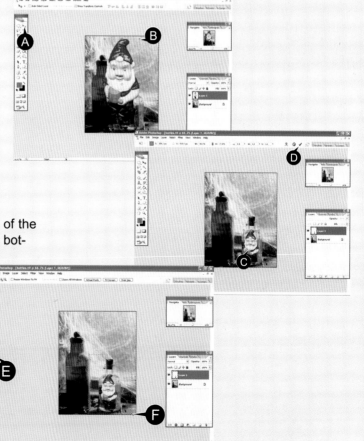

STEP 6 : ADDING PERSPECTIVE

To make the gnome look like it is within the bottle, we need to start by bringing the label in front of the gnome. To do this, we will create a selection that contains only the label, create a layer from that selection, and then bring it in front of the gnome.

A. Click the eye-shaped icon beside Layer 1 to hide the layer.

B. Click on the Background layer. It will be highlighted.

C. Click the Lasso Tool button.

D. Click the "New selection" button in the options bar.

E. Click and drag around the label to select it.

F. Press Ctrl+J (PC) or Command+J (Mac) to create a separate layer from the selection.

STEP 7 : SELECTING THE BOTTLE

We need to select the rest of the bottle and change the opacity levels to make things look realistic when we put the gnome in the bottle.

A. Click on the Background layer. It will be highlighted.

B. Click and drag around the bottle, except for the area that contains the label. When you release the mouse button, a selection marquee will appear.

C. Press Ctrl+J (PC) or Command+J (Mac) to create a separate layer from the selection.

D. Click the Opacity arrow to bring up a slider.

E. Drag the slider to 55%. When we put the gnome behind this layer, the gnome will show through.

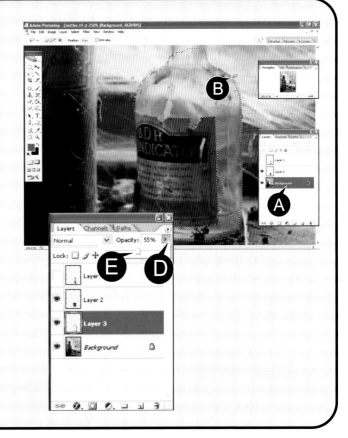

STEP 8 : MOVING THE LAYERS

To bring the gnome behind the other layers, we simply need to click and drag to move it.

A. Click the dimmed eye-shaped icon beside Layer 1 to make it visible again.

B. Click and drag Layer 1 downward until a black line appears above the Background layer. When you release the mouse button, the gnome will be behind the two layers you created earlier.

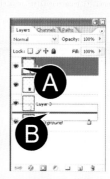

STEP 9 : DARKENING THE GNOME

We are going to make the gnome a little darker to make it look more realistic.

A. Click Image | Adjustments | Brightness/Contrast. The Brightness/Contrast dialog box will open.

B. Click and drag the sliders to enter the following settings: Brightness: -50, Contrast: 0.

C. Click OK. The settings will take effect.

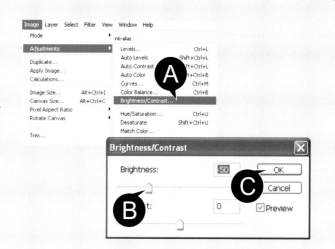

Need to get to a specific point in your image quickly? If so, press and hold the space bar to bring up the Hand tool. While the Hand tool is activated, you can click and drag in the direction you'd like to move, and the screen will shift.

Neon Sign

I used to attend a sign show every year as the staff member of a popular graphics application vendor. No matter what year it was, 80% of the questions I would receive involved how to create the illusion of neon in a graphic. Many of the attendees were sign manufacturers who needed to show their customers a preview of how a sign would look before it was actually created. By taking advantage of layer styles, you can apply a realistic neon effect to just about any object. Once the neon is applied, it can be tweaked to adjust the color and intensity.

Project Files

The file for this project is called neon.tif and can be found at: www.mimosabooks.com/files

Completion Time

After the files have been downloaded, this project should take approximately ten minutes to fifteen minutes to complete.

Degree of Difficulty

☆☆☆

Project Tools

▢ Rounded Rectangle Tool

✐ Eyedropper Tool

T Text Tool

➤ Move Tool

Palettes

Ensure the following palettes, which can be accessed from the Window menu, are open for this project:

Tools

Layers

STEP 1 : OPEN THE TUTORIAL

Before we can get any work done, we need to first open the file we'll need for this project.

A. Press Ctrl+O (PC) or Command+O (Mac) to launch the Open dialog box.

B. Browse to the folder where you saved the tutorial files.

C. Click on the file entitled "neon.tif." It will be high-lighted.

D. Click the Open button. The file will open.

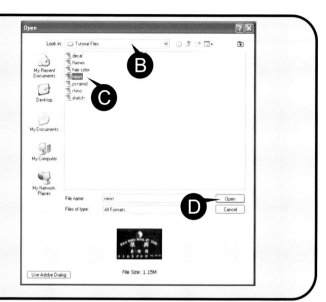

STEP 2 : CREATING THE SIGN

To create the sign we will use the Rounded Rectangle tool. Before we draw the rectangle, we'll choose the color for the sign. In most projects, we create a layer before we start editing; but in this case, a separate layer will automatically be created when you create the sign shape.

A. Double-click on the foreground color box, if the box itself is not already black. If it is black, you can skip to Step D.

B. Click on the color "black" or enter O in the H, S, and B fields.

C. Click OK. The foreground color will now be black.

D. Click and hold the Rectangle Tool button. A list of different tools will appear.

E. Click the Rounded Rectangle Tool option.

F. Click and drag a rounded rectangle over the set of three Chinese symbols. If you make a mistake or your sign doesn't look quite right, you can press Ctrl+Z (PC) or Command+Z (Mac) to undo your shape so that you can try again.

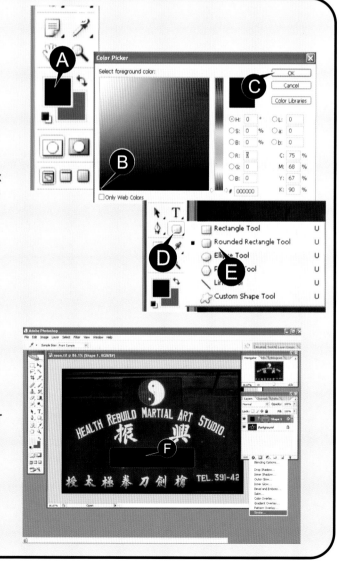

STEP 3 : CREATING THE OUTLINE

We're going to give the sign a yellow neon outline, but we want to match the yellow from the rest of the text in the sign. To do this, we'll use the Eyedropper tool. We'll then use a layer style to create the neon effect.

A. Click the Eyedropper Tool button.

B. Click on a symbol or text. The color of that text will now be loaded as the foregound color.

C. Click the "Add a layer style" button. A menu will appear.

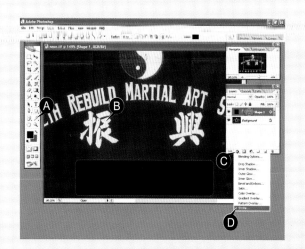

D. Click Stroke. The Stroke dialog box will appear.

E. Change the size to 7px.

F. Click the Fill Type drop-down and select Gradient, if it is not already selected.

G. Click on the long rectangle box with a gradient in it. The Gradient Editor dialog box will appear. We will now create our own gradient.

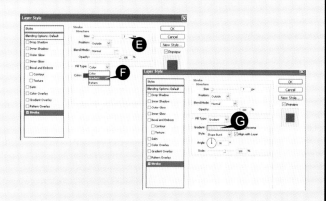

H. Click once at the bottom right side of the bar. You'll know you are at the proper spot because your mouse pointer will change into a little hand. A color stop will appear where you click.

I. Repeat Step H two more times in different areas on the line so that there are now a total of five color stops.

J. Double-click on the very first color stop. The Color Picker dialog box will appear.

K. Click on the color "black" or enter 0 in the R, G, and B fields.

L. Click OK. The first color stop will be black.

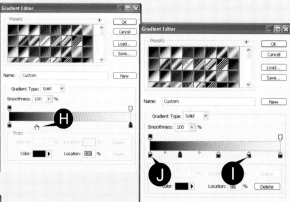

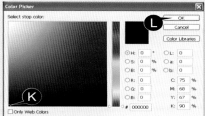

STEP 3 :CREATING CONT.

M. Repeat steps J - K for the color stop to the far-
thest right.

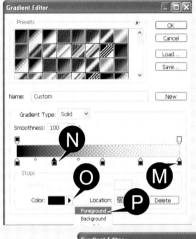

N. Click once on the second tab stop. A little arrow
will appear above the tab stop.

O. Click the arrow beside Color. A menu will appear.

P. Click Foreground. The foreground color that we
selected earlier with the Eyedropper tool will be inserted at the selected color stop.

Q. Repeat Steps O - P for the 3rd color stop.

R. Double-click on the middle tab stop. The Color
Picker dialog box will appear.

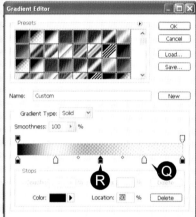

S. Click on the color "white" or enter 255 in the R, G,
and B fields.

T. Click OK. The middle color stop will be white.

U. Type the word "Neon" in the name box.

V. Click on the New button. The pattern you created
will be saved as a preset and can be accessed again
later.

W. Click OK. The Gradient Editor dialog box will
close.

X. Click on the Style drop-down button and select
Shape Burst.

Y. Click and drag the Opacity slider to 100%.

Z. Click OK. The sign will
now have a neon yellow border.

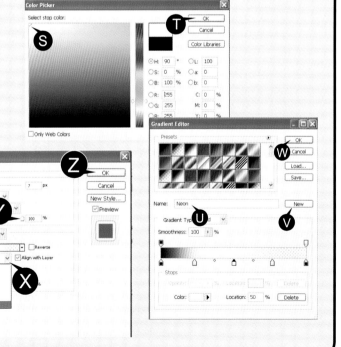

STEP 4 : CREATING LETTERS

Before we can make our letters on our sign appear in neon, we must first create the letters themselves.

A. Click the Eyedropper Tool button.

B. Click on any black area within the sign you created earlier.

C. Click the Text Tool button.

D. Click once on the image anywhere above the sign. A new text layer will appear, and a flashing cursor will appear on the screen.

E. Type "48" for the font size in the options bar.

F. Click the font drop-down and select Arial as the font. If you don't happen to have Arial, choose any other font.

G. Type the word you would like to use for your sign. Depending on the word you type, you may have to adjust the font size so that it will fit on the sign.

H. Click the Move Tool button. A series of handles (little boxes) will appear around the word you typed.

I.   Click and drag the letters over the sign. Since the letters are black and the sign is black, you will not be able to see the letters once they are over the sign. You will, however, be able to still see the handles that surround the text. In the next step, you'll be making these letters glow like neon.

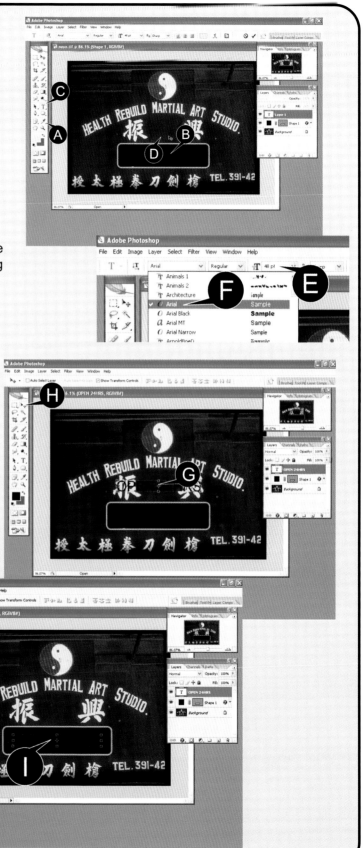

STEP 5: CREATING NEON LETTERS

The process for creating neon letters is very similar to that of creating the neon sign. We simply apply a layer style to the letters.

A. Click the "Add a layer style" button. A menu will appear.

B. Click Stroke. The Stroke dialog box will appear.

C. Enter 5px for the size.

D. Click the Fill Type drop-down button and select Gradient if it is not already selected.

E. Click on the narrow, long rectangle box with a gradient in it. A menu will appear.

F. Scroll through the Presets window until you get to the neon gradient you created earlier. It should be the last swatch in the list.

G. Click on the Neon swatch that you saved earlier. The pattern will be loaded.

H. Repeat Step E to close the window.

I. Click the Style drop-down arrow and select Shape Burst. We won't close this dialog just yet, because in the next step, we'll use it to make the letters glow.

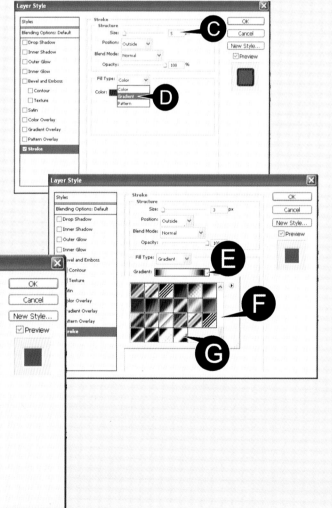

STEP 6 : GLOWING TEXT

The final step to making the word look like it is truly neon is to give it a slight glow. Once again, we'll be using a layer style to create this effect.

A. Click on the Outer Glow option in the Layer Style dialog box.

B. Click and drag the Opacity slider until it reaches 52%.

C. Click and drag Spread slider until it reaches 36%.

D. Click and drag the Size slider until it reaches 18px.

E. Click on the Color box. The Color Picker dialog box will appear.

F. Click on a yellow hue range.

G. Click on a light shade of yellow in the window.

H. Click OK. The Color Picker dialog box will close.

I. Click OK in the Layer Style dialog box. Your text will now have a slight glow to it.

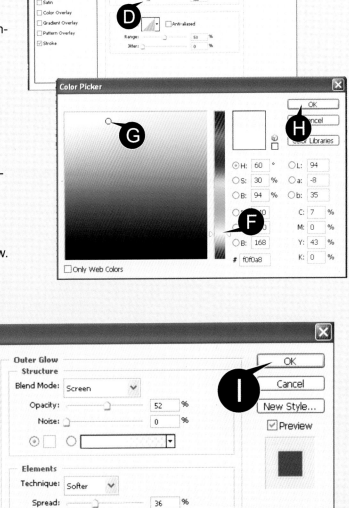

Turn A Photo Into A
Sketch

23

Project Files

The file for this project is called sketch.tif and can be found at:
www.mimosabooks.com/files

Completion Time

After the files have been downloaded, this project should take approximately five minutes to complete.

Degree of Difficulty

☆

Project Tools

This project uses only filters so there are no tools required.

Palettes

No windows or palettes are needed for this project.

If you're a TV junkie like me, you may recall a show from the early '90s called Blossom. Just prior to going to a commercial break, the show would freeze, and the frozen image would be converted to a sketch. That's exactly what we'll be doing in this project. We'll take a photograph, and, following a few steps, we'll convert our image into a colored sketch. This project makes use of several of the built-in filters of Photoshop. These filters allow you to apply a myriad of special effects to your images. With a bit of tweaking, you can convert just about any photograph to a colored sketch. In this project, we'll be converting an image of a flag; but the technique also works very well with pictures of landscapes, flowers, and abstracts.

STEP 1 : OPEN THE TUTORIAL

Before we can get any work done, we need to first open the file we'll need for this project.

A. Press Ctrl+O (PC) or Command+O (Mac) to launch the Open dialog box.

B. Browse to the folder where you saved the tutorial files.

C. Click on the file entitled "sketch.tif." It will be highlighted.

D. Click the Open button. The file will open.

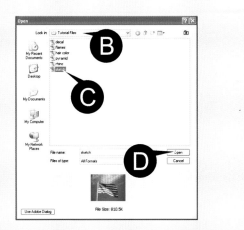

STEP 2 : CREATING NEW LAYER

Rarely should you ever work on your original image. The best practice is to make a copy of your original image on a separate layer and conduct your editing on the copy. That way, if you make a tragic mistake, your original image is not affected.

A. Press Ctrl+J (PC) on the keyboard or Command+J (Mac) to create a duplicate of the Background layer. By default, the new layer will be selected. The new layer, called "Layer 1" will appear. Since this project will ultimately have several layers, we will give this layer a new name so that it is easier to keep track of.

B. Double-click on the layer name. It will become highlighted and now will be editable.

C. Type the word "Outline" for the layer.

D. Press the Enter or Return key. The layer will now have its new name.

E. Click on the layer called "Background" so that it is highlighted.

F. Repeat Steps A - D to create one more copy of the Background layer. Rename this layer "Fill". You should now have a total of three layers.

G. Click on the Outline layer to select it, as we will begin work on that layer.

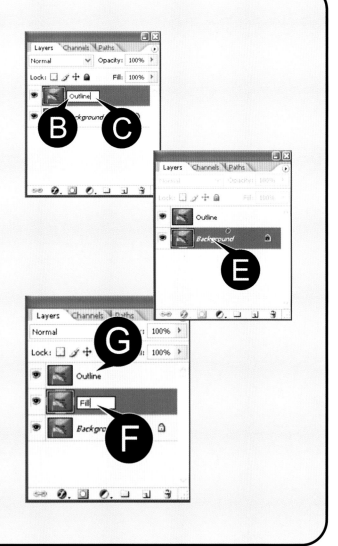

STEP 3 : CREATING THE OUTLINE

One of the main characteristics of sketches is that the objects drawn in them have dark outlines that are filled in with shading. In this step, we'll create those dark outlines, by using several of the filters that are included in Photoshop.

A. Click Filter | Stylize | Glowing Edges. A dialog box will appear from which you can adjust the settings of this filter.

B. Enter the following values in their respective boxes: Edge Width: 4, Edge Brightness: 3, and Smoothness: 6.

C. Click OK. The effect will be applied to the image. You will see that the image now has a black background with a colored outline of the flag. We'll need to invert this to get the look we are going for.

D. Click Ctrl+I (PC) or Command+I (Mac) to invert the image. We now have a rough outline sketch of our image. To soften the edges of the sketch, we'll use the Gaussian Blur filter.

E. Click Filter | Blur | Gaussian Blur. The Gaussian Blur dialog box will appear.

F. Enter "1.0" for the radius of the blur.

G. Click OK. The blur will be applied to the layer.

H. Click Shift+Ctrl+U (PC) or Command+Shift+U (Mac) to desaturate (take all the colors out) of the layer.

I. Click Image | Adjustments | Brightness/Contrast to launch the Brightness/Contrast dialog box.

J. Drag the Contrast slider until the level is 40 then click the OK button.

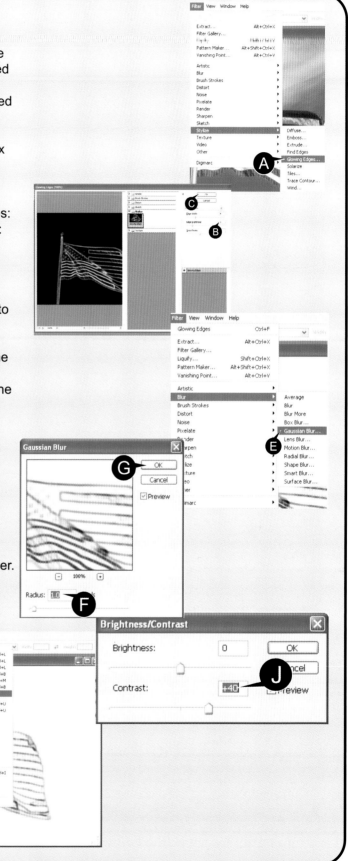

STEP 4 : BLENDING THE LAYERS

The next step is to blend the rough sketch outline with the solid image underneath. We will use the Multiply option, which will remove the white in the image and slightly change the color of the outline.

A. Click the Blend Mode drop-down arrow to see a list of different blending options.

B. Click Multiply. The "Outline" layer will now be blended with the "Fill" layer.

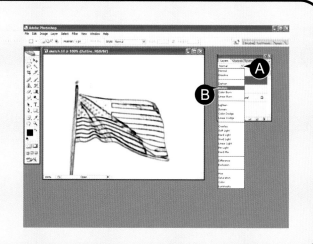

NOTES

STEP 5 : FILLING THE IMAGE

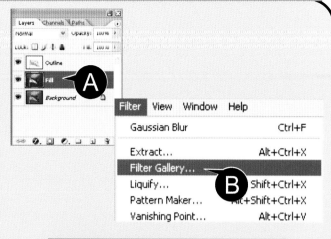

Now that we have the outline created, we need to create the fill. To make the fill look like a sketch, we'll take advantage of several filters. To apply the filter, we'll take advantage of the Filter Gallery (only in version CS and CS2), which allows us to apply multiple filters all in one shot. If you are using Photoshop 7, you will have to apply these filters individually.

A. Click on the "Fill" layer. It will now be highlighted to indicate that it is selected.

B. Click Filter | Filter Gallery. This will open the Filter Gallery that will allow you to apply multiple effects to an image all at once.

C. Click the drop-down menu and select Paint Daubs.

D. Enter the following values: Brush Size: 9, Sharpness: 0, and Brush Type: Wide Blurry.

E. Click the New Effect layer button. You will now be able to apply another effect to the image.

F. Click the drop-down menu and select Film Grain.

G. Enter the following values: Grain: 5, Highlight Area: 5, and Intensity: 1.

H. Click the New Effect layer button. You will now be able to apply another effect to the image.

I. Click the drop-down menu and select Smudge Stick.

J. Enter the following values: Stroke Length: 5, Highlight Area: 0, and Intensity: 5.

K. Click OK. The effect will be applied to the image. Ta da! You've now converted your photo to a colored sketch.

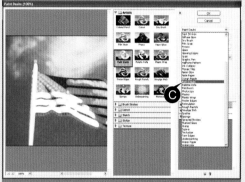

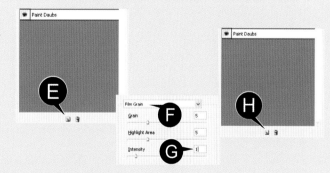

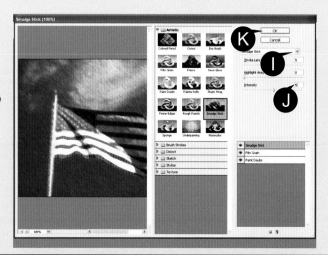

Change Of Scene

Project Files

The file for this project is called sky.tif and can be found at: www.mimosabooks.com/files

Completion Time

After the files have been downloaded, this project should take approximately ten minutes to fifteen minutes to complete.

Degree of Difficulty

☆☆☆

Project Tools

🔍 Zoom Tool

🔧 Magic Wand Tool

🔗 Lasso Tool

Palettes

Ensure the following palettes, which can be accessed from the Window menu, are open for this project:

Tools

I recently had a pool installed at my house. And it's funny, because after the installation I have become an instant meteorologist. I always need to know what the forecast is so that I can plan out my activities. Wouldn't it be nice if we didn't need to be so dependent on the weather and we could change the forecast to suit our needs? The good news is that in Photoshop you can! In this project, we'll replace one sky with another. Rather than taking the new sky from an existing image, we will actually create it from scratch using Photoshop's Render Clouds feature. By creating a selection with the Magic Wand tool, we can remove the existing sky and put in our newly created background.

STEP 1 : OPEN THE TUTORIAL

Before we can get any work done, we need to first open the file we'll be using in this project.

A. Press Ctrl+O (PC) or Command+O (Mac) to launch the Open dialog box.

B. Browse to the folder where you saved the tutorial files.

C. Click on the file entitled "sky.tif." It will be highlighted.

D. Click the Open button. The file will open.

E. Click the Maximize button to expand the window to fit the screen.

F. Press Ctrl+0 (PC) or Command+0 (Mac) to fit the image to the screen.

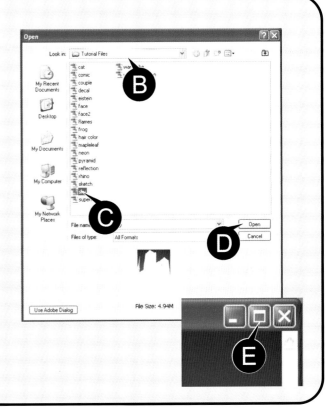

STEP 2 : CREATING A SELECTION

To replace the sky, we will need to create a selection. Because the background is fairly solid, we can make use of the Magic Wand tool, which allows us to select entire regions with similar colors.

A. Click the Magic Wand Tool button.

B. Type "50" into the Tolerance field in the options bar.

C. Uncheck any boxes. There should be no checks in any of the boxes in the options bar.

D. Click once on the sky. Most of the sky will be selected, but not all, so we'll continue selecting.

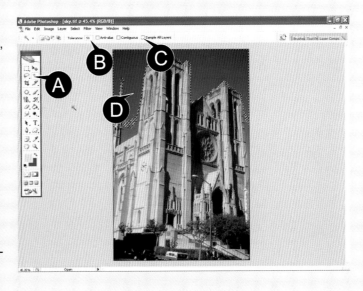

STEP 2 : CREATING CONT.

E. Click on the "Add to selection" button on the options bar.

F. Click on the area of the sky that is not selected. All of the sky will now be selected.

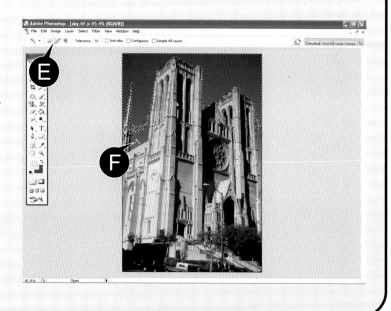

STEP 3 : TIDYING UP

The Magic Wand tool selects color ranges. You have the option of selecting contiguous colors. However, we did not so that parts of the background peeking through the windows would also be selected. The problem is that other areas of blue in the picture were also selected. Therefore, we'll remove them using the "Subtract from selection" option on the options bar.

A. Click the Zoom Tool button.

B. Click and drag around an area that was included in the selection that isn't part of the background.

C. Click on the Lasso Tool button.

D. Click on the "Subtract from selection" button on the options bar.

E. Click and drag around any areas in the selection that were inadvertently selected. They will now be removed from the selection.

F. Press Ctrl+0 (PC) or Command+0 (Mac) to fit the image to the screen.

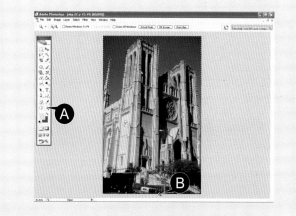

STEP 4 : CREATING THE SKY

To replace the background, we have several options. We can choose an existing image of a background, or, as in this case, we can create a sky from scratch.

A. Click Ctrl+N (PC) or Command+N (Mac) to open the New dialog box.

B. Type the following settings: Width: 942, Height: 1431, and Resolution: 300.

C. Click OK. The document will be created.

D. Click Filter | Render | Clouds. Clouds will be created in this document.

E. Press Ctrl+A (PC) or Command+A (Mac) to select the entire document. A marquee will appear around the image.

F. Press Ctrl+C (PC) or Command+C (Mac) to copy the image.

G. Click Window | sky.tif to switch back to the original image.

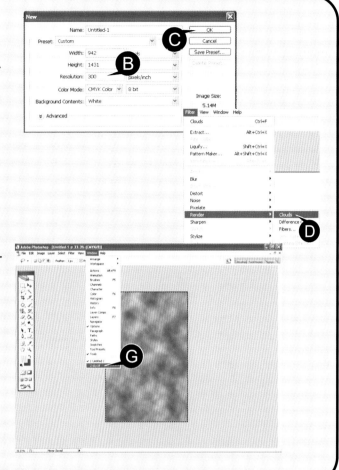

STEP 5 : FINALIZING

When you switch back to the image with the sky, you'll see that the selection that you made earlier is still active. We will now use the Paste Into command to insert the sky that we created into the background.

A. Click Edit | Paste Into. The clouds background will be inserted into the image. Your image will now have a new background.

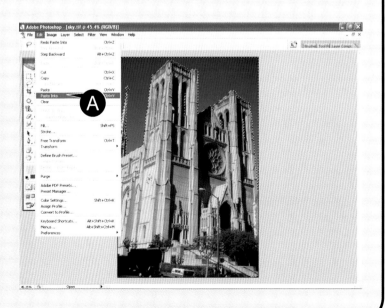

Monkey Face

Project Files

The files for this project are called monkey.tif and cheetah.tif and can be found at: www.mimosabooks.com/files

Completion Time

After the files have been downloaded, this project should take approximately five minutes to fifteen minutes to complete.

Degree of Difficulty

☆☆☆

Project Tools

Paint Bucket Tool

Clone Stamp Tool

Lasso Tool

Move Tool

Palettes

Ensure the following palettes, which can be accessed from the Window menu, are open for this project:

Tools

Who amongst us hasn't wanted to play the role of God -- being all-powerful and having the ability to create anything you'd like? In this project, you'll get to do some experimenting as if you were all-knowing and all-powerful. There are two keys to getting a realistic look to the animal. The first is that, when isolating the monkey's head, you capture parts of the fur on the face that are sticking out. To accomplish this, you will use the Extract feature that was first introduced in Photoshop CS. The second key is that you must resize and position the monkey's head so that it fits in perspective with that of the original animal. When you are finished, you should be left with your new species!

STEP 1 : OPEN THE TUTORIAL

Before we can get any work done, we need to first open the files we'll need for this project. You can open multiple files at the same time within Photoshop. The order in which you select the files will determine the order in which they open. The file you select first, will be the active file when the files open.

A. Press Ctrl+O (PC) or Command+O (Mac) to launch the Open dialog box.

B. Browse to the folder where you saved the tutorial files.

C. Click on the file entitled "monkey.tif." It will be highlighted.

D. Hold down the Ctrl key (PC) or Command key (Mac) and click on the file called "cheetah.tif." It too will now be selected.

E. Click the Open button. Both files will open, but the monkey file will be active because it was the first file selected.

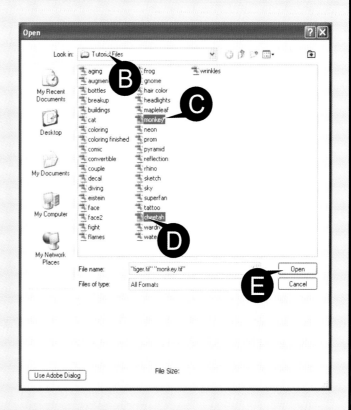

NOTES

STEP 2 : ISOLATING THE HEAD

Our goal is to isolate the monkey's head so that we can bring it into our picture of the cheetah. To do this, we are going to make use of the Extract feature. The Extract feature is not available in version 7, so if you are using that version, use the Lasso Tool to create a selection and jump to Step I below.

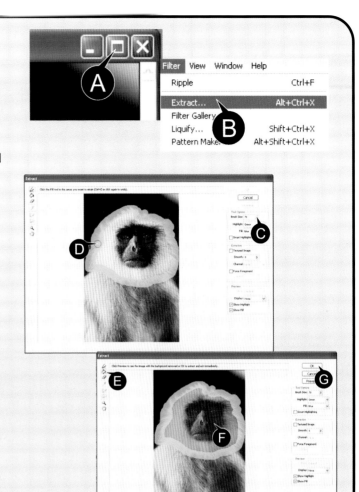

A. Click the Maximize button to expand the window. This will make it easier to isolate the monkey.

B. Click Filter | Extract. The Extract window will appear.

C. Set the brush size to 78, if it is not already set at that size.

D. Click and drag around the outside edge of the monkey's face. As you drag, a highlighted line will appear around where you drag.

E. Click on the Fill Tool button.

F. Click once inside the area that was outlined earlier in Step D. The monkey's entire face will be highlighted.

G. Click OK. Everything but the monkey's face will be transparent.

H. Press Ctrl+A (PC) or Command+A (Mac) to select the entire image.

I. Press Ctrl+C (PC) or Command+C (Mac) to copy the selection. We will later paste it.

J. Click Window | cheetah.tif to switch to the image of the cheetah.

K. Press Ctrl+J (PC) or Command+J (Mac) to create a copy of the cheetah image on a new layer.

L. Click the Maximize button to expand the window.

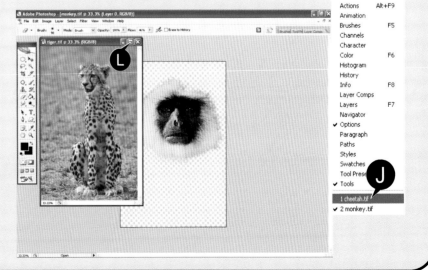

STEP 3 : REMOVING THE HEAD

Before we paste the monkey's head onto this image, we'll need to remove the head of the cheetah. Even though the monkey's head will be on top of the cheetah's, we want to make sure none of the cheetah's head peaks through the background, since the two heads aren't exactly the same size. To accomplish this we will use the Clone Stamp tool.

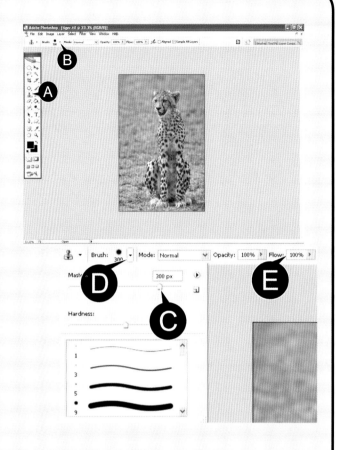

A. Click on the Clone Stamp Tool button.

B. Click on the Brush Preset picker arrow. A menu will appear where you can adjust the setting for the Stamp tool.

C. Click and drag the sliders to adjust the following settings: Master Diameter: 300px, and Hardness: 50%.

D. Repeat Step B to close the menu.

E. Type 100% in the Opacity box and 100% in the Flow box, if they are not already set at those levels.

F. Hold down the Alt key and click once to the left of the cheetah's head. This area will be used as the source for your clone.

G. Click several times over the cheetah's head. It will appear to be gone as the background area is cloned over it. Be sure just to click, not click and drag, as you conduct the clone.

STEP 4 : INSERTING THE MONKEY'S HEAD

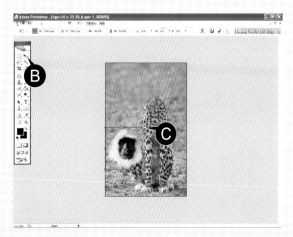

Because the monkey's head was copied to the clipboard, we simply need to paste it into our image. Once inserted, we'll resize it, to fit on the cheetah's head.

A. Press Ctrl+V (PC) or Command+V (Mac) to paste the monkey's head into the image.

B. Click the Move Tool button. A series of handle boxes will appear around the head.

C. Click and drag inward on any of the corner handles to resize the monkey's head. Resize it until it is about the size if the cheetah's head was before you cloned over it.

D. Position your mouse pointer over the middle of the monkey's face. Click and drag the head until it is on the cheetah's neck.

E. Click the Commit button. The monkey's head will now be on the cheetah's body.

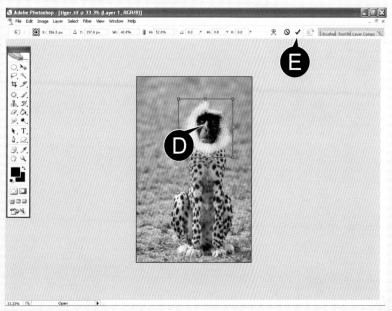

PHOTOGRAPHY 101

Act Natural - Rarely in life do people stand together, pose and smile when not taking photographs. For this reason your subjects don't need to be posed in every photo that you take. If you let your subjects act naturally you can get some very memorable shots that are different than the standard issue, stand together and smile photos. It may take a little longer to get the perfect shot, but the reward from the quality of photo you take will be worth it. This is especially true of photos that include children. Why have a child fake a pose and smile, when you can photograph them acting naturally and capture their true nature.

Extreme Diving

26

Project Files

The files for this project are called buildings.tif and diving.tif and can be found at: www.mimosabooks.com/files

Completion Time

After the files have been downloaded, this project should take approximately five minutes to fifteen minutes to complete.

Degree of Difficulty

Project Tools

Zoom Tool

Brush Tool

Palettes

Ensure the following palettes, which can be accessed from the Window menu, are open for this project:

Tools

Isn't it funny how every four years, whenever the Summer Olympics come along, we all of a sudden take interest in sports that we would never give a second thought to otherwise? Diving is one such sport for me; but I will say that, depending on the venue, you can get some spectacular views of the city from the top diving board. In this project, we are going to create the illusion of one of these spectacular views by transporting the image of the diver over a city scape. There are many different isolation techniques that we can use in Photoshop to remove an object from an image, and in this case, we'll be using a technique called layer masking.

STEP 1 : OPEN THE TUTORIAL

Before we can get any work done, we need to first open the file we'll be using in this project.

A. Press Ctrl+O (PC) or Command+O (Mac) to launch the Open dialog box.

B. Browse to the folder where you saved the tutorial files.

C. Click on the file entitled "buildings.tif." It will be highlighted.

D. Click the Open button. The file will open.

E. Click the Maximize button to expand the window to its full size.

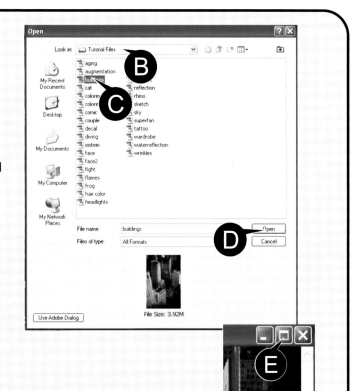

STEP 2 : BLURRING

We'll slightly blur the background to create the illusion of depth of field; but first, we'll duplicate the back-ground layer to create a working layer.

A. Press Ctrl+J (PC) or Command+J (Mac) to create a duplicate of the Background layer.

B. Click Filter | Blur | Box Blur. The Box Blur dialog box will open.

C. Type "8" in the Radius dialog box. The preview window will show you the new look of the image.

D. Click OK. The blur will be applied to the image.

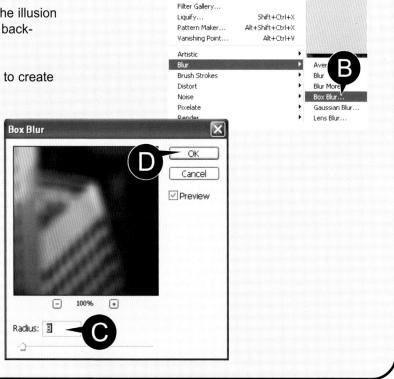

STEP 3 : IMPORTING THE DIVER

To bring the diver into the image, we'll use the Place command, which simply allows you to "place" another file into your image.

A. Click File | Place. The Place dialog box will open.

B. Click on the file "diving.tif." The file will be highlighted.

C. Click the Place button. The file will be imported into the current document.

D. Click the Commit button on the options bar.

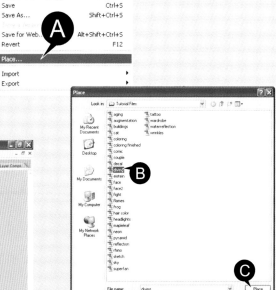

STEP 4 : CREATING A LAYER MASK

Of the many ways to remove a background in Photoshop, one of the fastest is to create a layer mask. Once you have a layer mask created, you can "paint" to remove or add parts of a background.

A. Click Layer | Layer Mask | Reveal All. The layer mask will be created. Nothing will appear to change on your image.

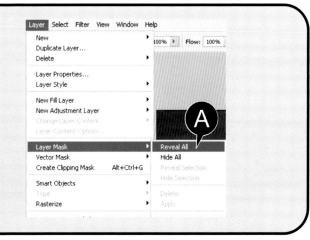

STEP 5 : BACKGROUND REMOVAL

Selecting the color black for the fill will remove elements of a background as you paint onto a layer mask, while using white will return any parts of the background that have been removed.

A. Click the "Set foreground color" box. A dialog box will appear from which you can select the foreground color.

B. Click on the color "black" or enter 0, 0, 0 in the R, G, and B fields.

C. Click OK. The foreground color will now be set.

D. Click the Brush Tool button.

E. Click the Brush Preset picker arrow. A menu with different options for the brush will appear.

F. Click and drag the sliders to set the following values: Master Diameter: 150px, Hardness: 0%.

G. Ensure that the other settings in the options bar are as follows: Opacity: 100%, Flow: 100%, and Mode: Normal.

H. Click and drag around the diver to remove most of the background. Get as close to her as possible, but don't worry about getting in too closely, because we'll take care of the fine edges in the next step.

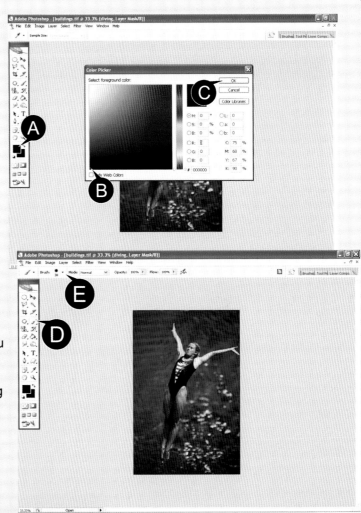

STEP 5 : REMOVAL CONT.

I. Repeat Steps E - F, this time entering the following values: Master Diameter: 30px, Hardness: 50%.

J. Click the Zoom Tool button.

K. Click and drag over any edge of the woman to zoom into an area where the background is still showing through.

L. Click the Brush Tool button.

M. Carefully click and drag around the edge of the woman. Don't worry if you go a little too far; you can always click Ctrl+Z (PC) or Command+Z (Mac) to undo your last command.

N. After you've finished tidying everything in the current view, hold down the Space bar, and click and drag to change the current view to see other areas where the background is still showing through. As the spacebar is held down, you'll notice that your mouse pointer has changed to the Hand tool.

O. Repeat Step M for other areas around the image until all of the background is removed.

P. Press Ctrl+0 (PC) or Command+0 (Mac) to zoom out of your image and see the results of your work.

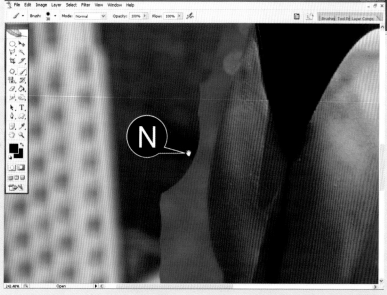

Hair Transplant

27

I'm sure that you've seen the ad for a popular hair restoration clinic, in which the spokesman says, "I'm not only the owner, I'm also a client." While there are literally hundreds of hair loss treatments on the market, none seem to work 100% -- except perhaps one. That one of course is Photoshop. In this project you'll simply be transplanting hair from one image to another. After we've copied and pasted the selection of hair, we'll reposition it on the photo of the man. Goodbye bald, hello bad wig!

Project Files

The files for this project are called bald.tif and hair.tif and can be found at: www.mimosabooks.com/files

Completion Time

After the files have been downloaded, this project should take approximately ten minutes to fifteen minutes to complete.

Degree of Difficulty

Project Tools

Zoom Tool

Magnetic Lasso Tool

Lasso Tool

Move Tool

Palettes

Ensure the following palettes, which can be accessed from the Window menu, are open for this project:

Tools

Layers

STEP 1 : OPEN THE TUTORIAL

Before we can get any work done, we need to first open the files we'll need for this project. You can open multiple files at the same time within Photoshop. The order in which you select the files will determine the order in which they open. The file that you select first will be the active file when the files open.

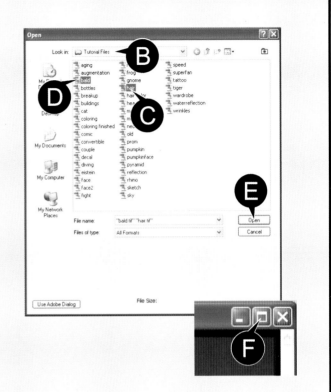

A. Press Ctrl+O (PC) or Command+O (Mac) to launch the Open dialog box.

B. Browse to the folder where you saved the tutorial files.

C. Click on the file entitled "hair.tif." It will be high-lighted.

D. Hold down the Ctrl key (PC) or Command key (Mac) and click on the file called "bald.tif." It too will now be selected.

E. Click the Open button. Both files will open, but the "hair" file will be active, because it was the first file selected.

F. Click the Maximize button to enlarge the window.

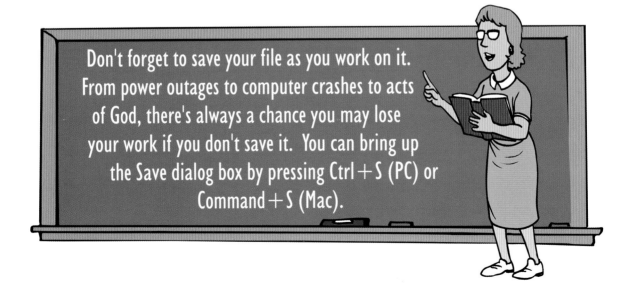

Don't forget to save your file as you work on it. From power outages to computer crashes to acts of God, there's always a chance you may lose your work if you don't save it. You can bring up the Save dialog box by pressing Ctrl+S (PC) or Command+S (Mac).

STEP 2 : ISOLATING THE HAIR

Our goal is to isolate the woman's hair so that we can transplant it into our picture of the bald man. To do this we are going to make use of the Magnetic Lasso tool.

A. Click the Zoom Tool button.

B. Click and drag around the woman's head. As you drag, a marquee will appear indicating the location of the new zoom level. When you release the mouse button, you will be zoomed to that point.

C. Click and hold the Lasso Tool button. A list of different selection tools will appear.

D. Click the Magnetic Lasso Tool option.

E. Enter "1" in the Feather box.

F. Click and drag around the outside edge of the woman's hair. As you drag, a line with little nodes on it will appear, previewing the location of your selection. You can also click in certain points around the outside of the hair to anchor the nodes. Don't worry if the line doesn't perfectly surround the hair, we'll make little adjustments later on in the process to perfect it.

G. Double-click once your line reaches the point where you started. A selection marquee will now appear around the hair.

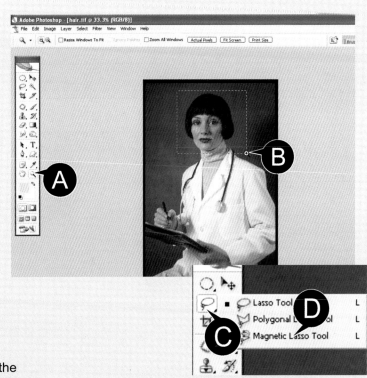

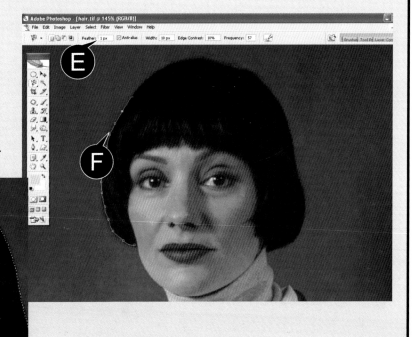

STEP 3 : TIDYING UP

The Magnetic Lasso tool did a great job of creating a selection around the hair, but it wasn't perfect. We can now add or take away from the selection using the Lasso tool.

A. Click and hold the Magnetic Lasso Tool button. A list of different selection tools will appear.

B. Click the Lasso Tool option.

C. Click the "Add to selection" button in the options bar. This will allow you to add areas to your selection.

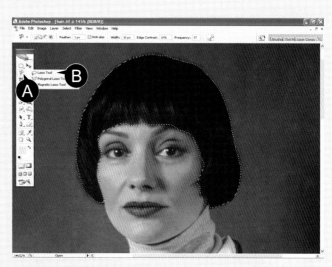

D. Click and drag around any areas of the hair that were not selected in your first selection attempt. When you release the mouse button, these areas will be selected.

E. Continue adding areas to the selection by clicking and dragging around them as required.

F. Click the "Subtract from selection" button on the options bar. This will allow you to remove areas from your selection.

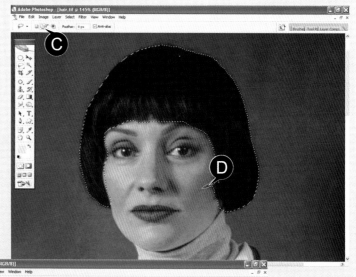

G. Click and drag around any areas of the head that are part of your selection that you would like to remove. When you release the mouse button, these areas will be removed from the selection.

H. Repeat Steps C through G until the hair is completely selected.

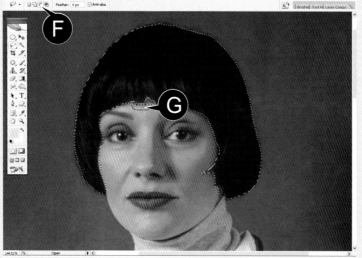

STEP 4 : TRANSPLANTING

To bring the hair into the image of the bald man, we will simply copy and paste it.

A. Press Ctrl+C (PC) or Command+C (Mac) to copy the hair to the system clipboard.

B. Click Window | bald.tif. This will switch the active window to the image of the man.

C. Click the Maximize button so that the image takes up the entire window.

D. Press the Ctrl+V (PC) or Command+V (Mac) to paste the hair into the image.

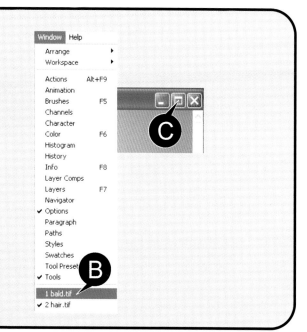

STEP 5 : RESIZING THE HAIR

We are now going to reposition and resize the hair so that it fits nicely on the man's head.

A. Click on the Move Tool button. A series of nodes will appear around the hair.

B. Position the mouse pointer over a corner node. Click and drag inward to resize the hair until it is the proper size for the man's head.

C. Position the mouse pointer over the middle of the hair. Click and drag until the hair fits on the man's head.

D. Click the Commit button on the options bar.

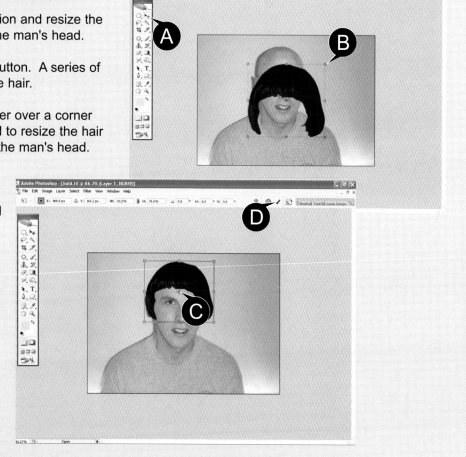

STEP 6 : ADDING PERSPECTIVE

To make the hair look more realistic, we are going to bring the man's ear in front of the hair. To do this, we will create a selection that contains only the man's ear. We will then create a layer from that selection and bring it in front of the image.

A. Click the eye-shaped icon beside Layer 1, which contains the hair, to hide the layer.

B. Click on the Background layer. It will be highlighted.

C. Click the Lasso Tool button.

D. Click the "New selection" button in the options bar.

E. Click and drag around the man's right ear to select it.

F. Press Ctrl+J (PC) or Command+J (Mac) to create a separate layer from the selection.

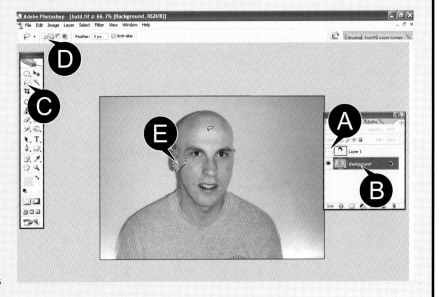

STEP 7 : MOVING THE LAYERS

To bring the hair behind the other layers, we simply need to click and drag to move it.

A. Click the dimmed eye-shaped icon beside Layer 1 to make it visible again.

B. Click and drag Layer 1 downward, until a black line appears above the Background layer. When you release the mouse button, the hair will be behind the man's ear.

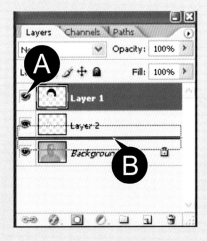

STEP 8 : LIGHTENING THE HAIR

The original picture that contained the hair was quite a bit brighter than the image of the man. To fix this, we will simply adjust the brightness of the layer that contains the hair.

A. Click Image | Adjustments | Brightness/Contrast. The Brightness/Contrast dialog box will open.

B. Click and drag the sliders to enter the following settings: Brightness: +40, Contrast: -2.

C. Click OK. The settings will take effect.

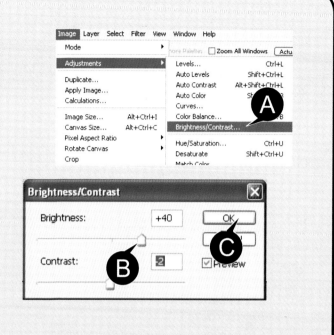

NOTES

Operation
Rhino
Drop

Project Files

The files for this project are called rhino.tif and pyramid.tif and can be found at: www.mimosabooks.com/files

Completion Time

After the files have been downloaded, this project should take approximately fifteen minutes to twenty minutes to complete.

Degree of Difficulty

☆☆☆

Project Tools

⬚ Move Tool

⬚ Magnetic Lasso Tool

⬚ Lasso Tool

Palettes

Ensure the following palettes, which can be accessed from the Window menu, are open for this project:

Tools
Navigator
Layers

For those of you who are old enough to remember, you may recall a Disney movie from 1995 entitled "Operation Dumbo Drop." In the movie, an army troop goes through a series of high jinks while trying to transport an elephant during the Vietnam War in order to retain the loyalty of a local village. It's much easier to move large animals in Photoshop than in real life. In this project, we'll take a picture of a rhinoceros in his local habitat and paste it into the Egyptian pyramids. To make the photo more interesting, we'll make it seem as though the rhinoceros is gigantic and that it is stepping over the pyramid.

STEP 1 : OPEN THE TUTORIAL

Before we can get any work done, we need to first open the files we'll need for this project. You can open multiple files at the same time within Photoshop. The order in which you select the files will determine the order in which they open. The file that you select first will be the active file when the files open.

A. Press Ctrl+O (PC) or Command+O (Mac) to launch the Open dialog box.

B. Browse to the folder where you saved the tutorial files.

C. Click on the file entitled "rhino.tif." It will be high-lighted.

D. Hold down the Ctrl key (PC) or Command key (Mac) and click on the file called "pyramid.tif." It too will now be selected.

E. Click the Open button. Both files will open, but the rhino file will be active because it was the first file selected.

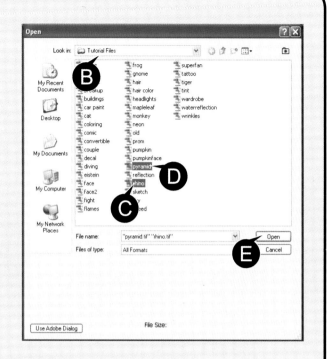

STEP 2 : PREPARING TO ISOLATE

Our goal is to isolate the middle rhinoceros so that we can bring it into our pyramid picture. To do this, we are going to make use of the Magnetic Lasso tool.

A. Click the Maximize button to expand the window. This will make it easier to isolate the rhinoceros.

B. Click and hold the Lasso Tool button. A list of different selection tools will appear.

C. Click the Magnetic Lasso Tool option.

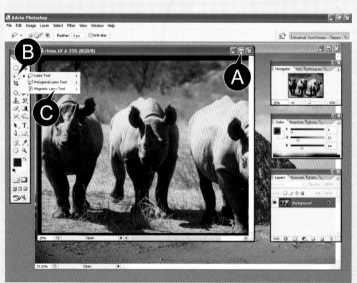

STEP 3 : ISOLATING

There are a myriad of ways to isolate an object in Photoshop. In this project, we'll make use of the Magnetic Lasso tool. This tool selects an area by attaching to the outline of an object, based on the object's contrast with the background.

A. Click and drag the Zoom slider in the Navigator palette until the middle rhinoceros takes up most of the screen. A zoom level of approximately 37% should accomplish this.

B. Click and drag around the outside edge of the rhinoceros. As you drag, a line with little nodes on it will appear, previewing the location of your selection. Don't worry if the line doesn't perfectly surround the rhinoceros; we'll make little adjustments later on in the process to perfect it.

C. Double-click once your line reaches the point where you started. A selection marquee will now appear around the rhinoceros.

By right-clicking anywhere on your image, you can bring up a menu of options associated with the tool you currently have selected. For example, if you right-clicked on the page when you had the Zoom tool selected, a menu with zoom options would appear.

STEP 4 : TIDYING UP

The Magnetic Lasso tool did a great job of creating a selection around the object, but it wasn't perfect. We can now add or take away from the selection using the Lasso tool.

A. Click and hold the Magnetic Lasso Tool button. A list of different selection tools will appear.

B. Click the Lasso Tool option.

C. Click the "Add to selection" button in the options bar. This will allow you to add areas to your selection.

D. Click and drag around any areas of the rhinoceros that were not selected in your first selection attempt. When you release the mouse button, these areas will be selected.

E. Continue adding areas to the selection by clicking and dragging around them as required.

F. Click the "Subtract from selection" button on the options bar. This will allow you to remove areas from your selection.

G. Click and drag around any areas of the rhinoceros that are part of your selection that you would like to remove. When you release the mouse button, these areas will be removed from the selection.

H. Repeat Steps C through G until the rhinoceros is completely selected.

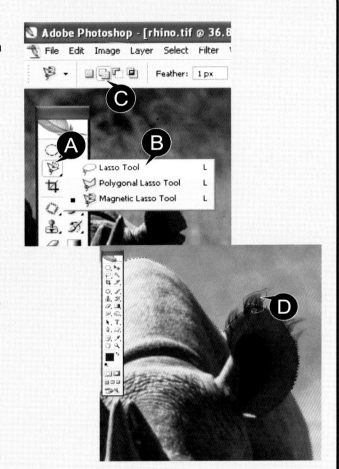

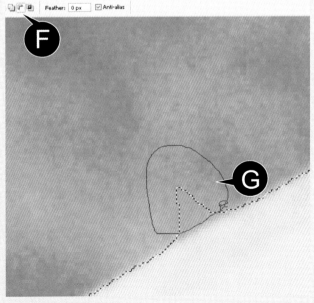

STEP 5 : TRANSPORTING

As discussed in the chapter introduction, "Operation Dumbo Drop" followed the story of an elephant that needed to be transported to a village in Vietnam to keep the loyalty of a native village. There were plenty of high jinks trying to transport such a large animal. There will be no such high jinks in your effort to transport the rhino to the pyramids, because it's simply a matter of cutting and pasting.

A. Press Ctrl+C (PC) or Command+C (Mac) to copy the selected rhinoceros to the system clipboard.

B. Click Window | pyramid.tif. This will switch the active window to the pyramid image.

C. Click the Maximize button so that the pyramid image takes up the entire window.

D. Press the Ctrl+V (PC) or Command+V (Mac) to paste the Rhino into the image.

STEP 6 : POSITIONING

We are now going to reposition the rhinoceros into the ideal location.

A. Click on the Move Tool button. A series of nodes will appear around the rhino.

B. Position the mouse pointer over the rhino. Click and drag the rhino to the left until it is positioned as seen in the accompanying image.

STEP 7 : PERSPECTIVE

The key to making the image look "real" is to make it seem as though the rhino is coming from behind the pyramids. To do this, we are going to replicate part of the pyramid and paste it over the rhinoceros's leg.

A. Click the Opacity arrow and drag the slider until it is at approximately 44%. This will make the rhino partially transparent so that we can see the pyramid underneath it.

B. Click on the Background layer in the Layers palette. It will appear highlighted.

C. Click on the Zoom Tool button. The mouse pointer will change to the Zoom tool.

D. Click and drag a marquee with the Zoom tool around the hind leg of the rhino. This will allow us to zoom in so that we can get a close look at the area to be replicated.

E. Click and hold the Lasso Tool button and click the Lasso Tool.

F. Click and drag to create a selection that hugs the side of the pyramid and encompasses the hind leg of the rhino.

G. Press Ctrl+C (PC) or Command+C (Mac) on the keyboard to copy the selection.

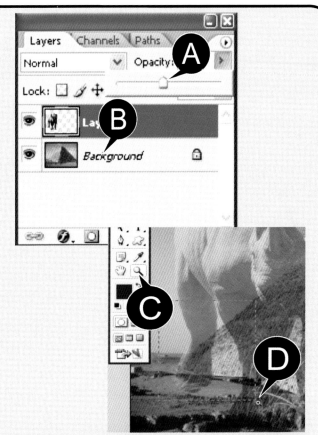

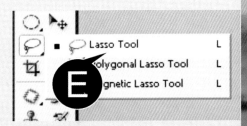

STEP 8 : PASTING THE SELECTION

Now we will paste the selection we have created on top of the hind leg of the rhino in order to create the illusion that the animal is stepping over the pyramids.

A. Click on the layer that contains the rhino in the Layers palette. It will be highlighted.

B. Click the Opacity arrow and drag the slider back up to 100%. The rhino will now appear solid on the image.

C. Press Ctrl+D (PC) or Command+D (Mac) to remove tho colcotion that was created in the last step.

D. Press Ctrl+0 (PC) or Command+0 (Mac) so that you can see the entire image.

E. Press Ctrl+V (PC) or Command+V (Mac) to paste the selection that will cover the hind leg of the rhino. The object will be pasted in the middle of your image.

F. Click on the Move Tool button. A series of nodes will appear around your object.

G. Position your mouse pointer over the object you just pasted. Click and drag the object over the hind leg of the rhino. It will now appear as if the rhino is stepping over the pyramid.

STEP 9 : COMBINING LAYERS

When you pasted your selections (the rhino and the corner of the pyramid), they were pasted onto individual layers. Now that you have finished with the image, you can combine all of the layers together.

A. Click Layer | Merge Visible. All visible layers will be merged together, and you will be left with your completed image.

Now Appearing In Color

Project Files

The file for this project is called coloring.tif and can be found at:
www.mimosabooks.com/files

Completion Time

After the files have been downloaded, this project should take approximately ten minutes to fifteen minutes to complete.

Degree of Difficulty

Project Tools

🔍 Zoom Tool

🪣 Paint Bucket Tool

🪢 Lasso Tool

Palettes

Ensure the following palettes, which can be accessed from the Window menu, are open for this project:

Tools

Layers

Colors

I'm sure at one point or another that you've walked past a photo-developing store in your local mall where they offered the service of having your old photos converted from black and white to color. Aside from the small fortune that you could save by doing it yourself, you'll find that Photoshop makes this process extremely easy. Once you get the hang of it, you can try hundreds of different color combinations to get colors that are right for you. This project uses several different coloring and selection techniques. The one that you ultimately end up using will depend on your preferences and the end result that you wish to see on screen.

STEP 1 : OPEN THE TUTORIAL

Before we can get any work done, we need to first open the files we'll need for this project.

A. Press Ctrl+O (PC) or Command+O (Mac) to launch the Open dialog box.

B. Browse to the folder where you saved the tutorial files.

C. Click on the file entitled "coloring.tif." It will be highlighted.

D. Click OK. The file will open.

E. Click the Maximize button to expand the window.

F. Press Ctrl+0 (PC) or Command+0 (Mac) to zoom to full view of the image.

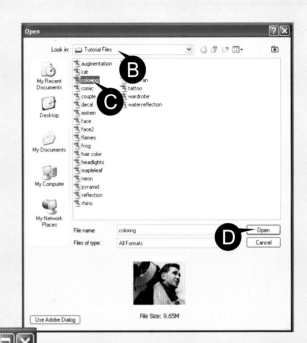

NOTES

STEP 2 : ISOLATING AREAS

Before we begin the process of coloring the photo, we need to isolate the specific area that we wish to apply color to. We'll do this by using the Lasso tool, which allows us to create a selection by simply drawing around the area that we would like to isolate.

A. Click the Zoom Tool button.

B. Click and drag around the man's face. As you drag, a marquee will appear, indicating the area for the zoom. When you release your mouse button, you will be zoomed in around the man's face. You may have to reposition your open palettes, if they are overlapping the man's face.

C. Click the Lasso Tool button.

D. Click the "New selection" button on the options bar, if it is not already selected.

E. Click and drag around the edge of the man's face and hair. When you release your mouse button, a series of "marching ants" will appear, indicating the area of the selection.

F. Click the "Add to selection" button in the options bar. This will allow you to add areas to your selection.

G. Click and drag around any areas that were not selected in your first selection attempt. When you release the mouse button, these areas will be selected. You may have to use the Zoom tool to get a close up view of certain areas. Keep in mind that after you've used the Zoom tool, you can always press Ctrl+0 (PC) or Command+0 (Mac) to see your full image again.

H. Continue adding areas to the selection by clicking and dragging around them as required.

I. Click the "Subtract from selection" button on the options bar. This will allow you to remove areas from your selection.

J. Click and drag around any areas that are part of your selection that you would like to remove. When you release the mouse button, these areas will be removed from the selection.

K. Repeat Steps F through J until the face and hair are completely selected.

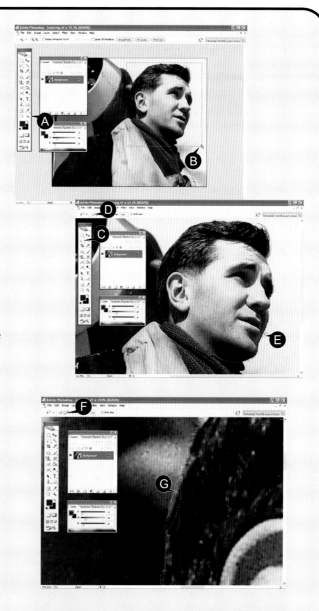

STEP 3 : USING VARIATIONS

The Variations command allows you to adjust the colors of a selection by slightly adjusting the hue levels. The beauty of the Variations command is that you can experiment with different color shades until you find the one you like.

A. Click Ctrl+J (PC) or Command+J (Mac) to make a layer from your selection.

B. Click Image | Adjustments | Variations. The Variations dialog box will open.

C. Click on any of the windows to add more color to your image. Experiment with different color levels. The window called "Current Pick" is a preview of how your image would look if you applied the colors you have adjusted.

D. Click on the window labeled "Original" to remove all the changes you've made and start over.

E. Click on the following windows in this order: twice on More Yellow and once on More Blue.

F. Click OK. The color within the selection will be adjusted.

G. Press Ctrl+0 (PC) or Command+0 (Mac) to see the full image.

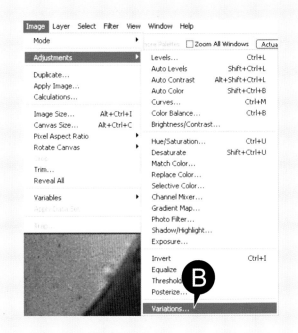

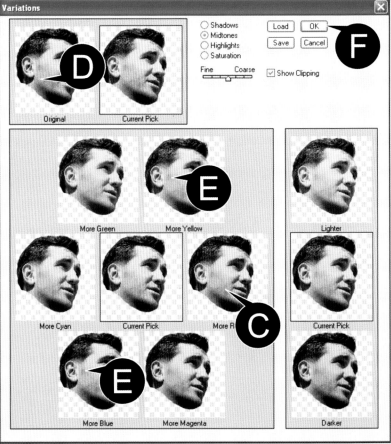

STEP 4 : FILLS AND BLENDS

The second method of coloring that we'll use involves applying a fill to an area and then changing the blend mode. A perfect tool for coloring a black and white image is the Color blend mode, which fades the fill that we apply to make it look realistic.

A. Click the New Layer button in the Layers palette. A new layer will be created.

B. Create a selection around the man's vest. Follow the instructions in Step 2 to create the selection.

C. Click on a yellow color in the Colors palette. This foreground color will change to the color you have selected.

D. Click the Paint Bucket Tool button.

E. Click anywhere within the selection. The selection will fill with the color that you chose in Step B.

F. Click the Blend Mode button in the Layers palette. A list of different blend modes will appear.

G. Click Color. The color in our selection will now fade into the image, and it will appear colorized.

H. Repeat Steps A - G for the man's scarf and jacket. You can choose to use the colors of your choice for those pieces.

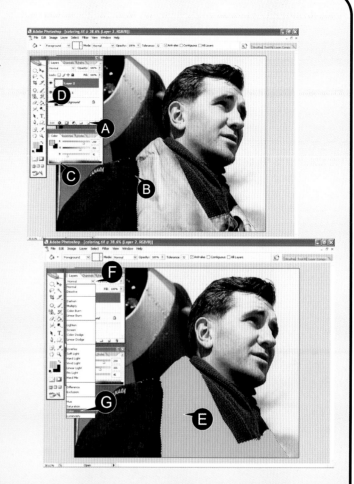

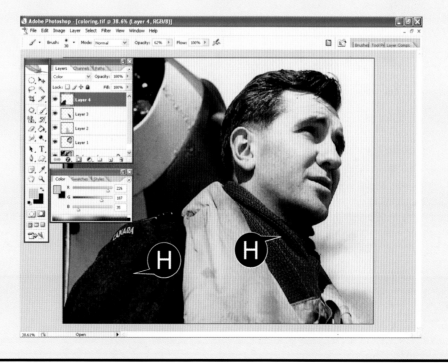

STEP 5 : COLORING WITH HUE

To color the sky in this image we, will use the Hue/Saturation command.

A. Create a selection that contains the sky. You can refer back to Step 2 for instructions on creating and adjusting a selection.

B. Click on the Background layer in the Layers palette.

C. Press Ctrl+J (PC) or Command+J (Mac) to create a layer that contains the selection.

D. Click Image | Adjustments | Hue/Saturation. The Hue/Saturation dialog box will open.

E. Click and drag the sliders to the following settings: Hue: +180, Saturation: +50, and Lightness: 0.

F. Click OK. The sky will now have a light-blue color.

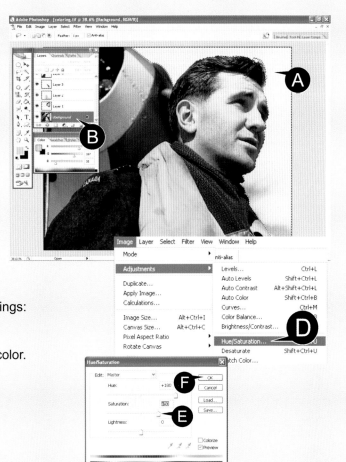

When working with more than one document at a time, you can take advantage of Photoshop's keyboard shortcuts. Pressing Ctrl + Tab will toggle you through your open documents.

STEP 6 : ADJUSTING HAIR COLOR

In an earlier step, we applied a color to the man's hair and face at the same time. For most people, hair color and skin color are not exactly the same, and this man is no exception. To differentiate the tone of the hair from that of the skin, we will change the brightness and contrast of the hair.

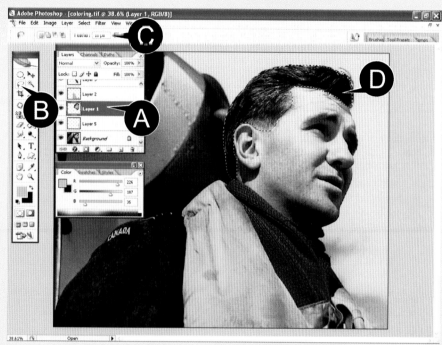

A. Click on Layer 1 in the Layers palette. This should be the layer that contains only the man's head.

B. Click the Lasso Tool button.

C. Type "10" in the Feather box in the options bar.

D. Click and drag around the man's hair to create a selection. Don't worry if your selection isn't perfect, because we've created a highly feathered edge.

E. Click Image | Adjustments | Brightness/Contrast. This will open the Brightness/Contrast dialog box.

F. Click and drag the sliders to set the following levels: Brightness: -40, Contrast: -30.

G. Click OK. The hair will now be several shades different from the face.

H. Press Ctrl+D (PC) or Command+D (Mac) to deselect the selection.

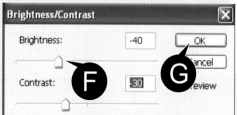

See Yourself In
Pumpkin

30

Have you ever wondered how people create those incredible, life-like carvings out of their pumpkins at Halloween? Well, wonder no longer -- it's really quite simple. You can take just about any photograph and convert it to a black and white image that can be used as a template when carving a pumpkin. In this project, you'll not only create a template, you'll also apply the template to a picture of a pumpkin so that you can preview how it will look before you start carving. Say goodbye to simple triangle eyes and zig-zagged mouth pumpkins. During this Halloween, your jack-o-lantern will be the envy of the block.

Project Files

The files for this project are called pumpkin.tif and pumpkinhead.tif and can be found at:
www.mimosabooks.com/files

Completion Time

After the files have been downloaded, this project should take approximately five minutes to ten minutes to complete.

Degree of Difficulty

Project Tools

 Move Tool

Magic Wand Tool

Lasso Tool

Palettes

Ensure the following palettes, which can be accessed from the Window menu, are open for this project:

Tools

Layers

STEP 1 : OPEN THE TUTORIAL

Before we can get any work done, we need to first open the files we'll need for this project. You can open multiple files at the same time within Photoshop. The order in which you select the files, will determine the order in which they open. The file you select first, will be the active file when the files open.

A. Press Ctrl+O (PC) or Command+O (Mac) to launch the Open dialog box.

B. Browse to the folder where you saved the tutorial files.

C. Click on the file entitled "pumpkinhead.tif." It will be highlighted.

D. Hold down the Ctrl key (PC) or Command key (Mac) and click on the file called "pumpkin.tif." It too will now be selected.

E. Click the Open button. Both files will open, but the pumpkinhead file will be active, because it was the first file selected.

F. Click the Maximize button to enlarge the window.

G. Press Ctrl+0 (PC) or Command+0 (Mac) to zoom to full view.

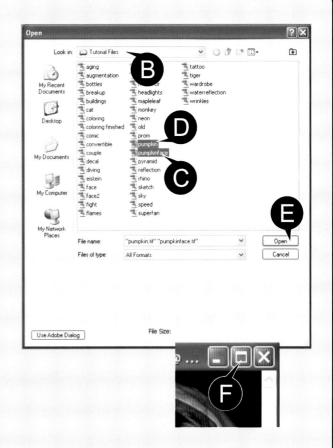

NOTES

STEP 2 : CONVERTING THE IMAGE

To make the image into something we can use for a template to cut our pumpkin, we need to first remove all the color and then adjust the levels.

A. Click Image | Adjustments | Desaturate. All the color will be removed from the image.

B. Click Image | Adjustments | Levels. The Levels dialog box will appear.

C. Enter the following numbers in the Input Levels box 107, 1.00 and 109.

D. Click the OK button to close the dialog box. You will be left with a black and white image that can be used as a template on your pumpkin.

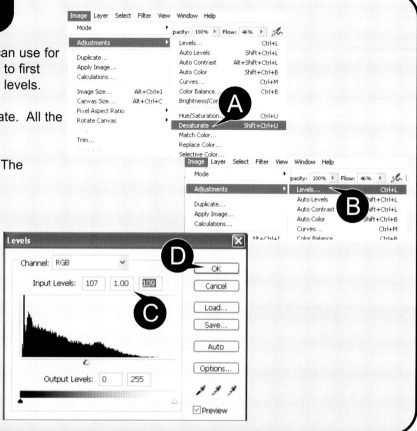

STEP 3 : SELECTING THE FACE

We are now going to select part of the woman's face to bring over to the pumpkin image so that we can preview how it'll look once we start carving.

A. Click the Lasso Tool button.

B. Click the "New selection" button in the options bar, if it's not already selected.

C. Enter "0" in the Feather box in the options bar.

D. Click and drag around the woman's face. Don't worry about being too accurate.

E. Press Ctrl+C (PC) or Command+C (Mac) to copy the selection.

F. Click Window | pumpkin.tif to switch to the pumpkin image.

STEP 4 : PLACING THE FACE

We are now going to paste the face image onto the pumpkin and resize it.

A. Click the Maximize button so that the pumpkin image takes up the entire window.

B. Press the Ctrl+V (PC) or Command+V (Mac) to paste the face into the image.

C. Click on the Move Tool button. A series of nodes will appear around the face.

D. Position the mouse pointer over the middle of the face. Click and drag it until it's right over the pumpkin.

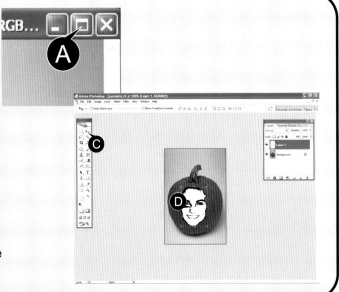

STEP 5 : BLENDING THE FACE

To get a good idea of how the face will look on the pumpkin, we'll blend the layers together using one of the blend modes.

A. Click the Blend Mode drop-down arrow to see a list of blend options.

B. Click the Lighten option.

C. Click the Magic Wand Tool button.

D. Ensure the Contiguous button is not checked in the options bar.

E. Click on any white area of the face. The white area will be selected.

F. Click the Delete layer button in the Layers palette.

G. Click Yes if you are prompted to confirm the deletion.

H. Press Ctrl+J (PC) or Command+J (Mac) to create a layer from the selection.

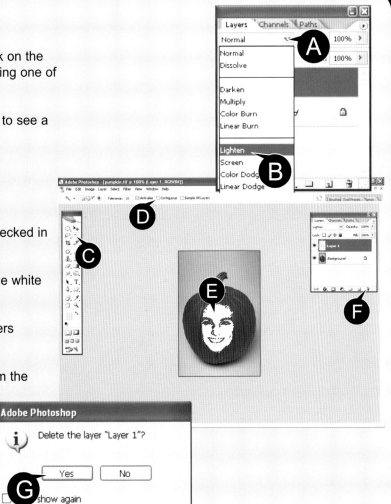

STEP 6 : ADJUSTING THE COLOR

We are going to adjust the color of the layer to make it look more like the interior of a lit pumpkin.

A. Click Image | Adjustments | Hue/Saturation. The Hue/Saturation dialog box will open.

B. Click and drag the settings as follows Hue: 30, Saturation: 50, Lightness: 50.

C. Click OK. The dialog box will close, and the settings will be applied. You can now see the face in the pumpkin.

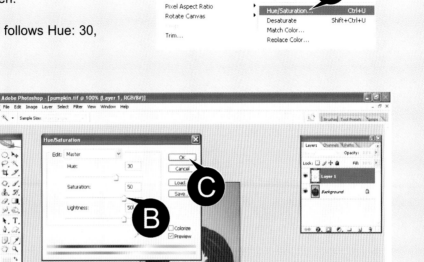

PHOTOGRAPHY 101

Don't Be A Statue - What do you do if the lighting isn't quite right, the background is busy, or you can't seem to get everything into the shot? It may sound quite simple, but so many people forget that one of the easiest ways to get a better shot is to move. The difference between a mediocre shot and a perfect image is sometimes just a matter of location. By changing your viewpoint, you can dramatically change the outcome of your picture.

KISS Cat

31

Project Files

The file for this project is called cat.tif and can be found at: www.mimosabooks.com/files

Completion Time

After the files have been downloaded, this project should take approximately ten minutes to fifteen minutes to complete.

Degree of Difficulty

☆☆☆

Project Tools

Move Tool

Lasso Tool

Polygon Lasso Tool

Palettes

Ensure the following palettes, which can be accessed from the Window menu, are open for this project:

Tools
Navigator
Layers

You can tell at first glance that this cat wants to "...rock and roll all night, and party every day.." The best part of this project is that you take advantage of the Liquify feature that allows you to make the cat appear as though it is smiling. Think of the Liquify feature as giving you the ability to convert your photo paper into a gel-like substance that can easily be molded. Through simple copy and pasting you are going to also make the cat appear as if it has a mohawk. We'll also make our cat look like Paul Stanley of KISS by applying a star to its eye. After you finish this project I suggest that you experiment with the Liquify feature on other photos of animals and people, it's guaranteed to give you hours of entertainment.

STEP 1 : OPEN THE TUTORIAL

Before we can get any work done, we need to first open the file we'll be using in this project.

A. Press Ctrl+O (PC) or Command+O (Mac) to launch the Open dialog box.

B. Browse to the folder where you saved the tutorial files.

C. Click on the file entitled "cat.tif." It will be highlighted.

D. Click the Open button. The file will open.

E. Click the Maximize button. The window will expand to fill the screen.

F. Click and drag the Zoom slider in the Navigator palette to approximately 64%.

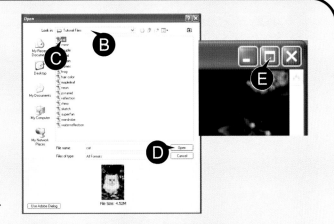

NOTES

STEP 2 : PREPARATION

As always, we are going to start by making a copy of the image, so that we don't inadvertently edit the original image. From there, we'll take advantage of the Liquify effect to make our cat smile.

A. Press Ctrl+J (PC) or Command+J (Mac) to make a copy of the image on a new layer.

B. Click Filter | Liquify. The Liquify dialog box will open.

C. Type the following values for the brush settings. Brush Size: 37, Brush Density: 75, Brush Pressure: 100.

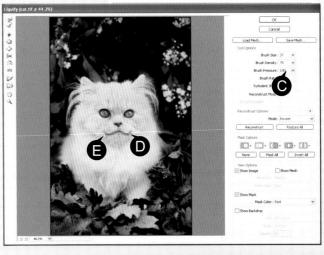

D. Starting from the middle of the cat's mouth, click and drag to the right and slightly upward until it appears that the cat is smiling.

E. Repeat Step D for the other side of the cat's mouth.

F. Position the mouse pointer at the top right of the cat's eye. Click and drag upward and to the right slightly.

G. Repeat Step F for the other eye.

H. Click OK. The effect will be applied to the cat.

STEP 3 : CREATING A SELECTION

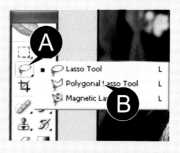

To create the star over the cat's eye, we'll start by making a selection that we'll color later. We don't want the selection to include the eye of the cat, so after the initial creation, we'll use the "subtractive mode" to remove the area around the eye.

A. Click and hold the Lasso Tool button. A list of options will appear.

B. Click the Polygonal Lasso Tool option.

C. Click once just to the right of the cat's eye.

D. Drag the mouse upward and to the left. As you drag, you'll see a line following the mouse pointer.

E. Click once to set an anchor point for the line.

F. Drag downward and to the left to create the first section of the star.

G. Continue clicking around the eye of the cat to create the shape of a star.

H. Double-click once you've reached the starting point, and a selection will be made.

I. Click and hold the Polygon Lasso Tool button. A list of options will appear.

J. Click the Lasso Tool option.

STEP 3 : CREATING CONT.

K. Click the "Subtract from selection" button from the options bar.

L. Click and drag around the cat's eye. When you release the mouse button, the area around the eye will be removed from the selection.

STEP 4 : FILLING THE SELECTION

We'll be putting the contents of the selection on its own layer so that we can later blend it with other layers to create the effect we are looking for.

A. Press Ctrl+J (PC) or Command+J (Mac) to create a new layer that contains only the contents of the selection.

B. Click Image | Adjustments | Hue/Saturation. The Hue/Saturation dialog box will open.

C. Click and drag the Lightness slider until it is at -50. Make sure the other two boxes have zeros in them.

D. Click OK. The effect will be applied to the layer.

E. Click on the Blend Mode drop-down arrow.

F. Click Multiply. The blend mode will be applied.

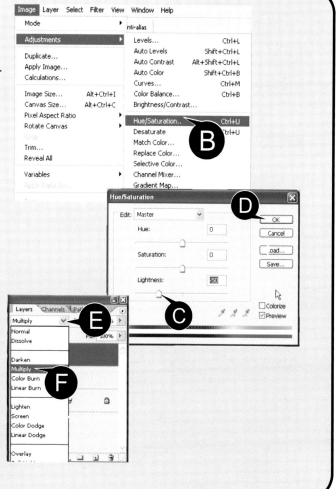

STEP 5 : CREATING THE MOHAWK

To create a little spiked hair style for the cat, we'll use some of its existing hairs. We'll then copy and paste them to a new layer.

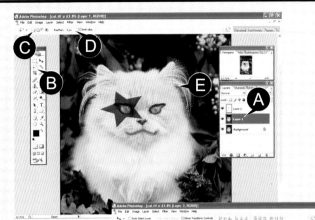

A. Click on Layer 1.

B. Click the Lasso Tool button.

C. Click the "New selection" button on the options bar.

D. Enter "3" in the Feather box.

E. Click and drag around the hair on the right side of the cat's face that sticks out slightly. When you release your mouse button, a selection will be created.

F. Press Ctrl+J (PC) or Command+J (Mac) to create a new layer out of your selection.

G. Click the Move Tool button. A series of handles will appear around the selection.

H. Position your mouse pointer just below and to the right of the bottom right handle. You'll know you're over the right position when the mouse pointer turns into a double-sided curved arrow.

I. Click and drag upward. As you drag, the selection will rotate.

J. Position the mouse pointer over a corner handle. Click and drag outward slightly to increase the size of the hair.

K. Position your mouse pointer over the middle of the selection. Click and drag to move the selection to the cat's head.

L. Press the Commit button on the options bar to commit the object. Just like that, you've got a punk rock cat.